The waves and other similar images presented herein, provide a variety of un-retouched photos of water being sloshed in a two-inch deep cooking pan on a summer's afternoon. I am curiously attracted to mathematic nonlinear chaotic images, both those that reveal organization (attractors) and those that produce apparent disorganization (chaos). The occasional multiple images of the sun's reflection and the various scratches and stains on the metal holding the water make, for me at least, a kind of code that enhances rather than detracts from the resultant images.

Waves

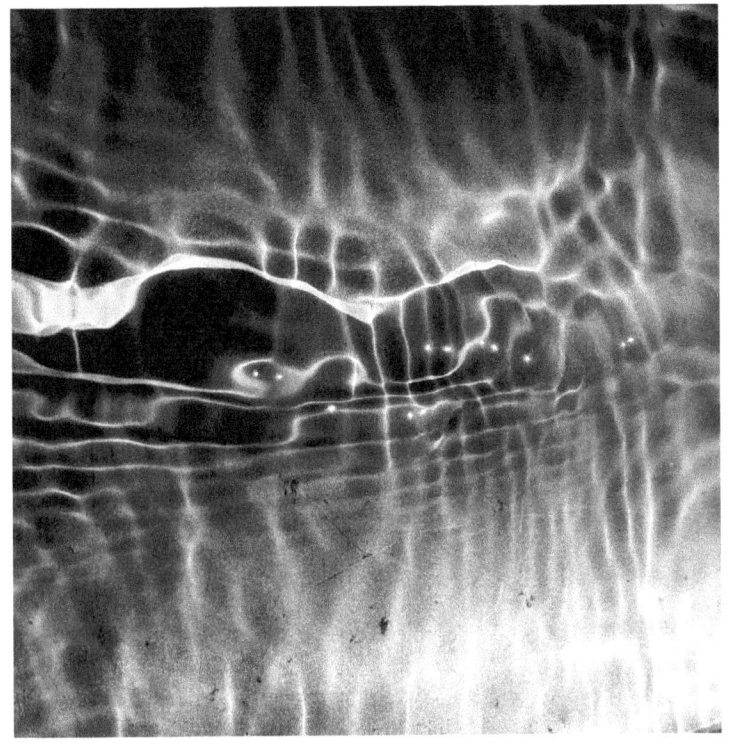

Photographs
By
David Cope

Waves

Photographs by David Cope

Epoc Books
Printed in the United States of America
© David Cope 2017
All Rights Reserved.
Published 2017.

This book is dedicated to my wife, sons, and grandchildren, Zoe, Tess, Gavin, and Ethan whose excitement for everyday things never ceases to amaze me. And to those older kids like me who believe in those children.

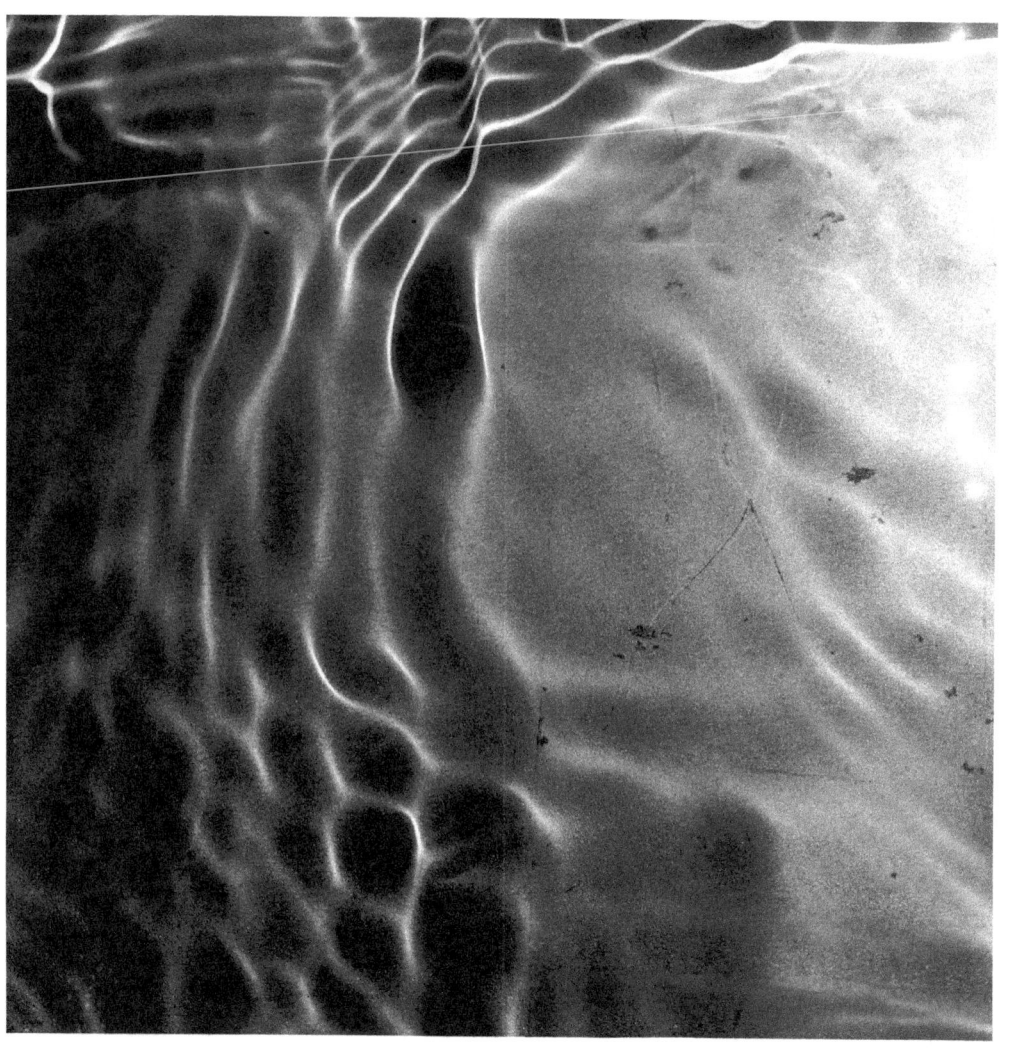

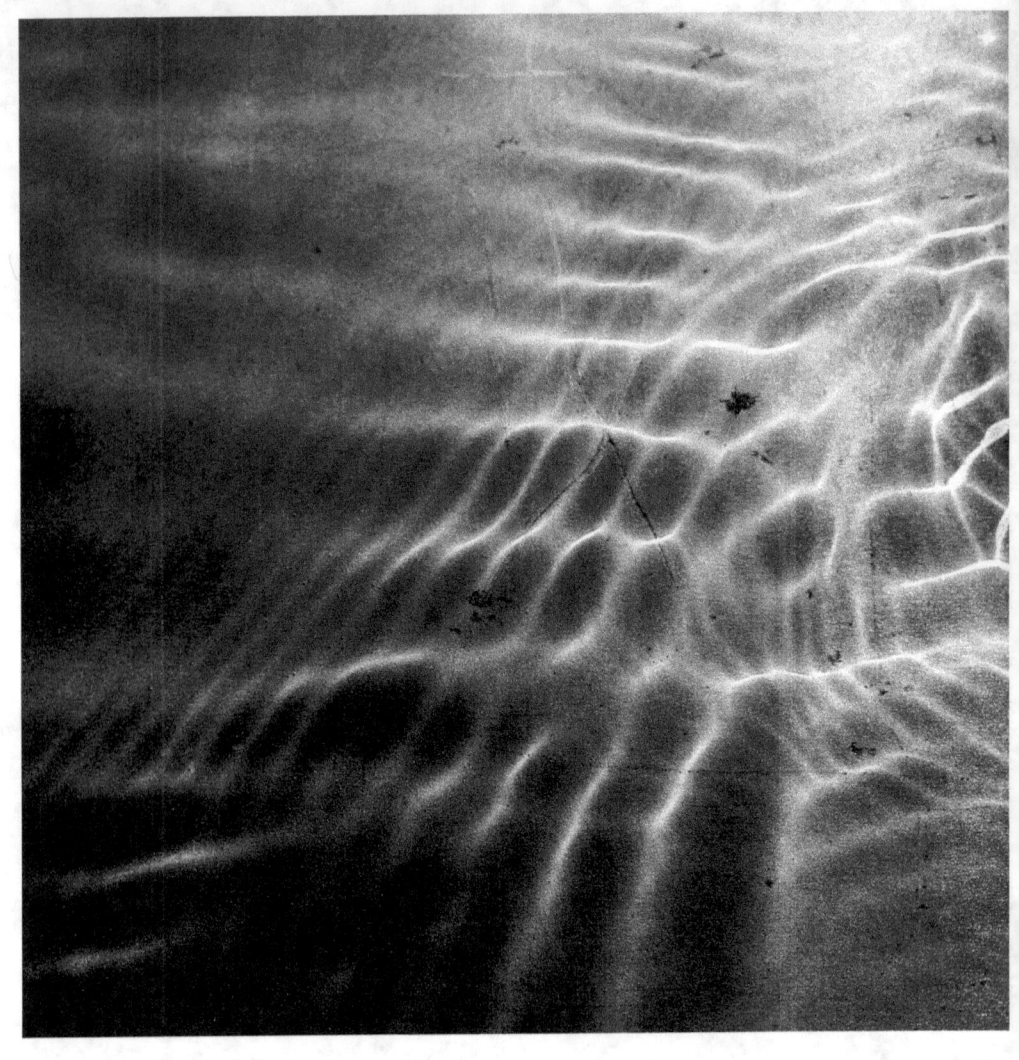

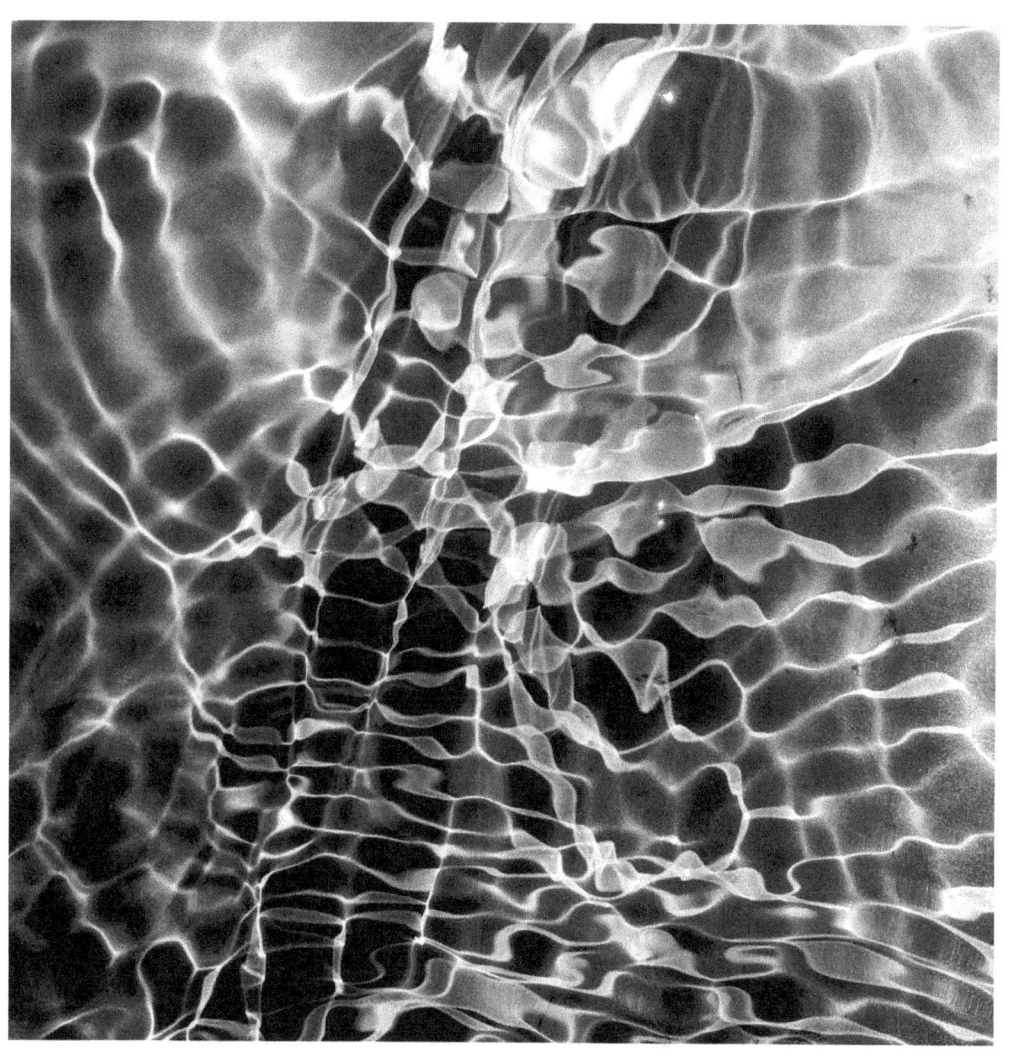

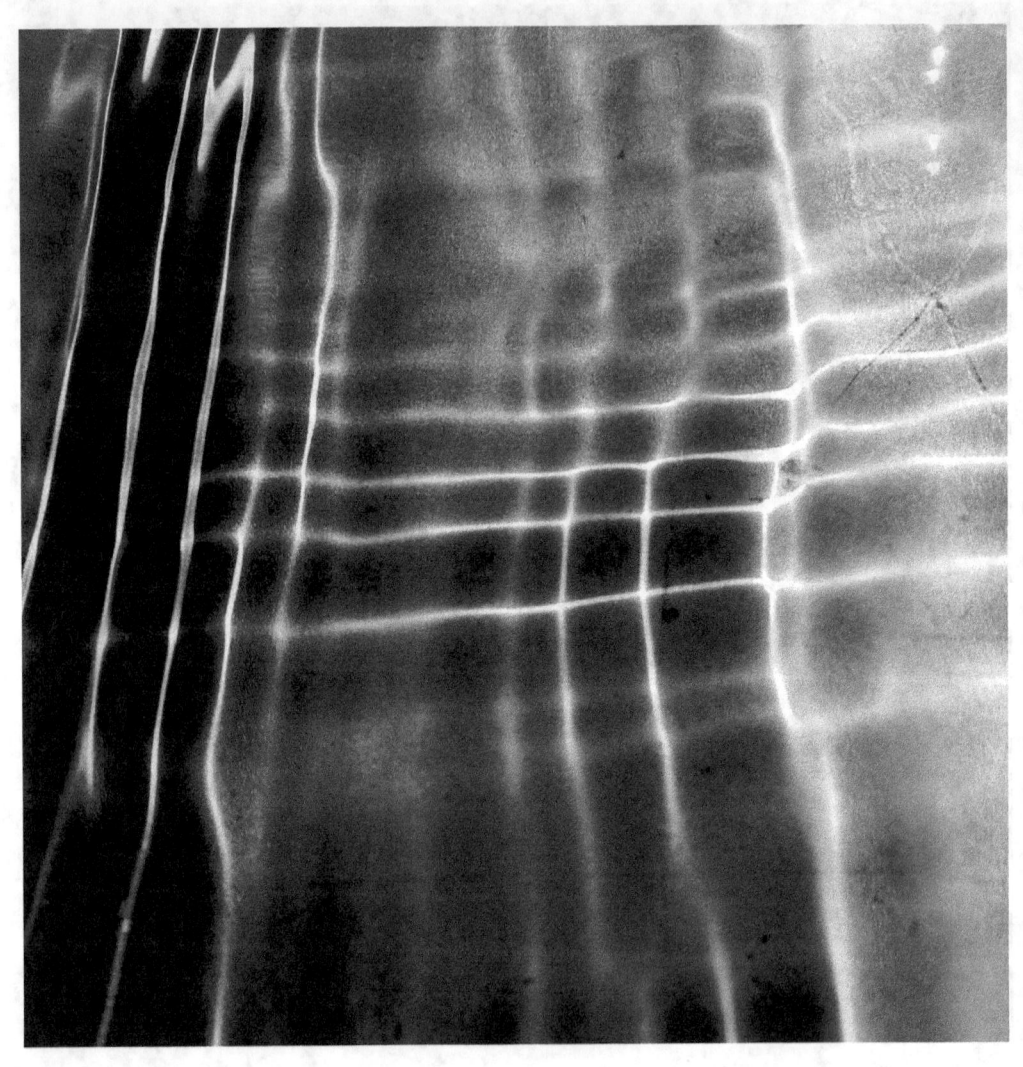

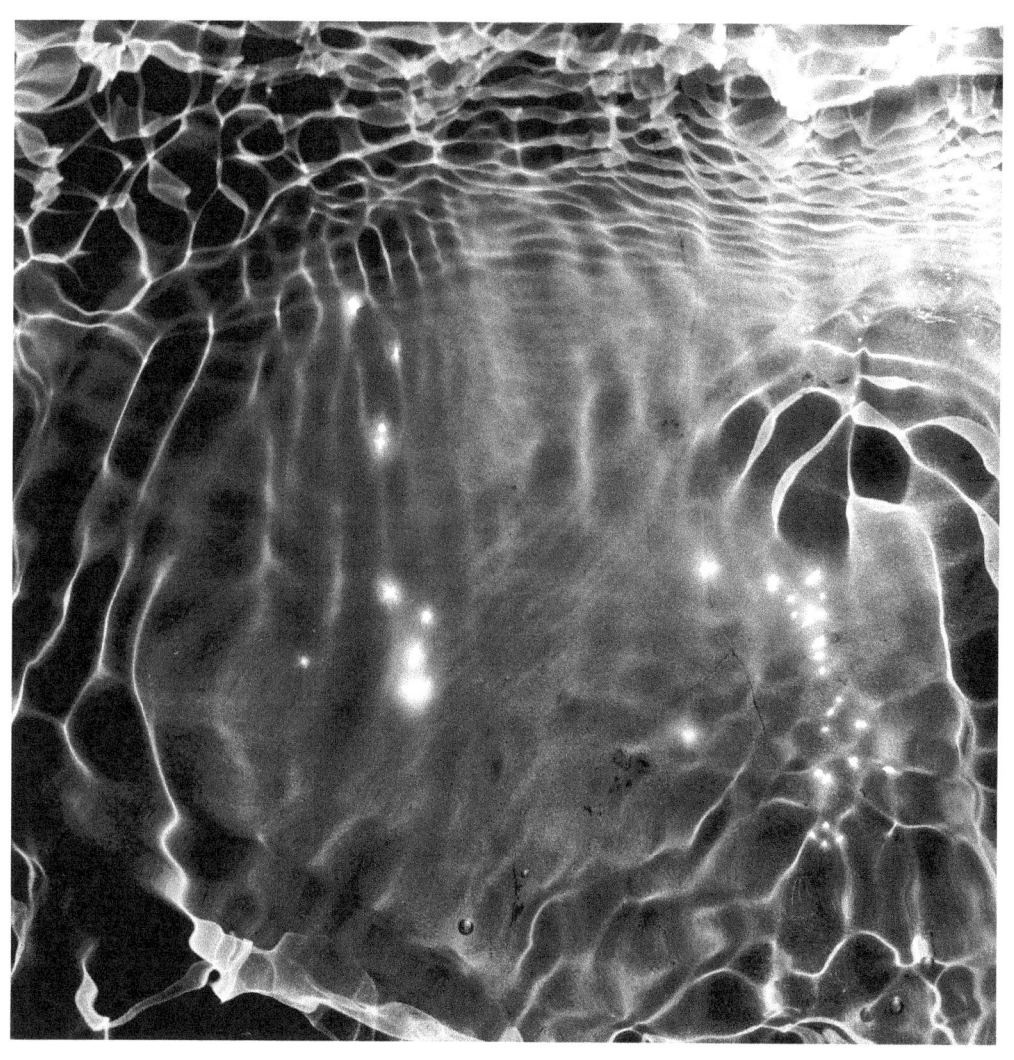

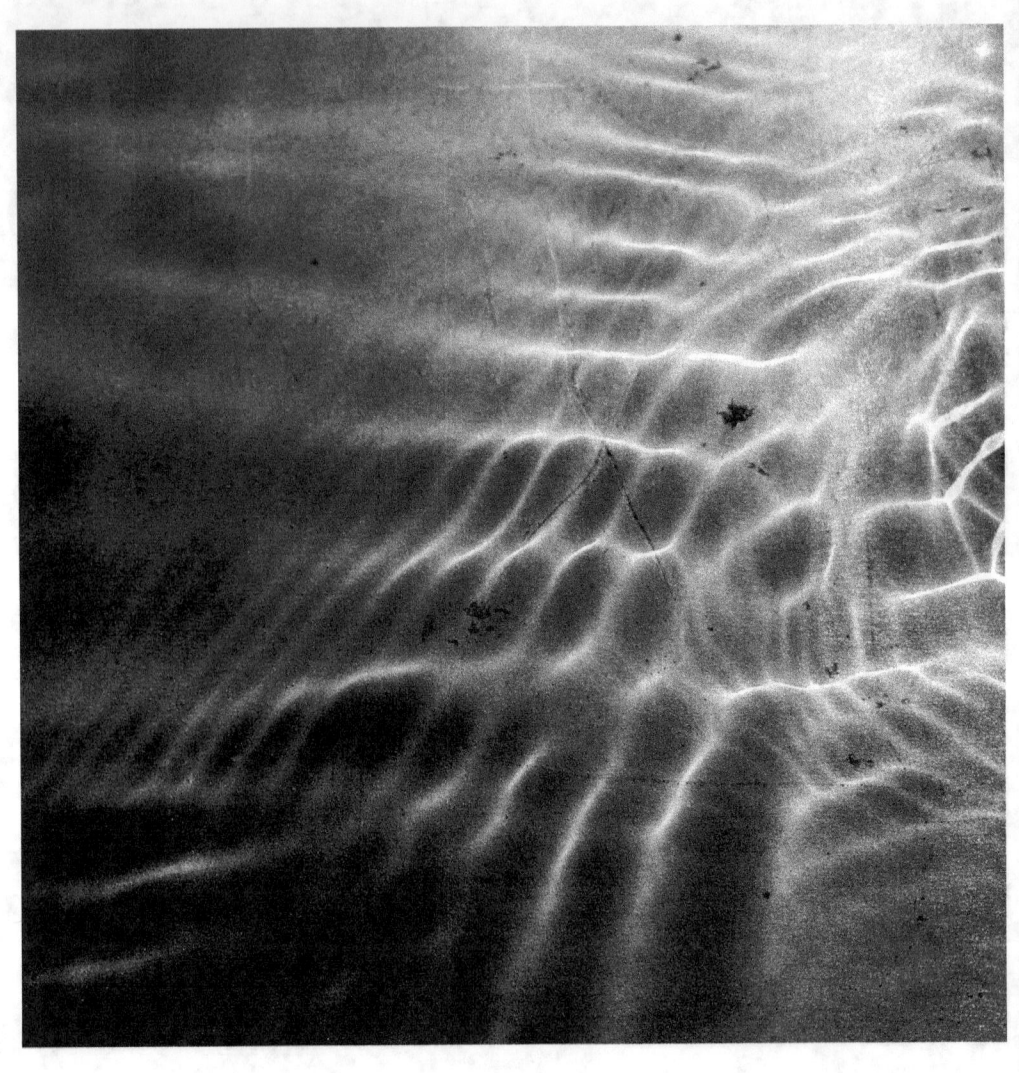

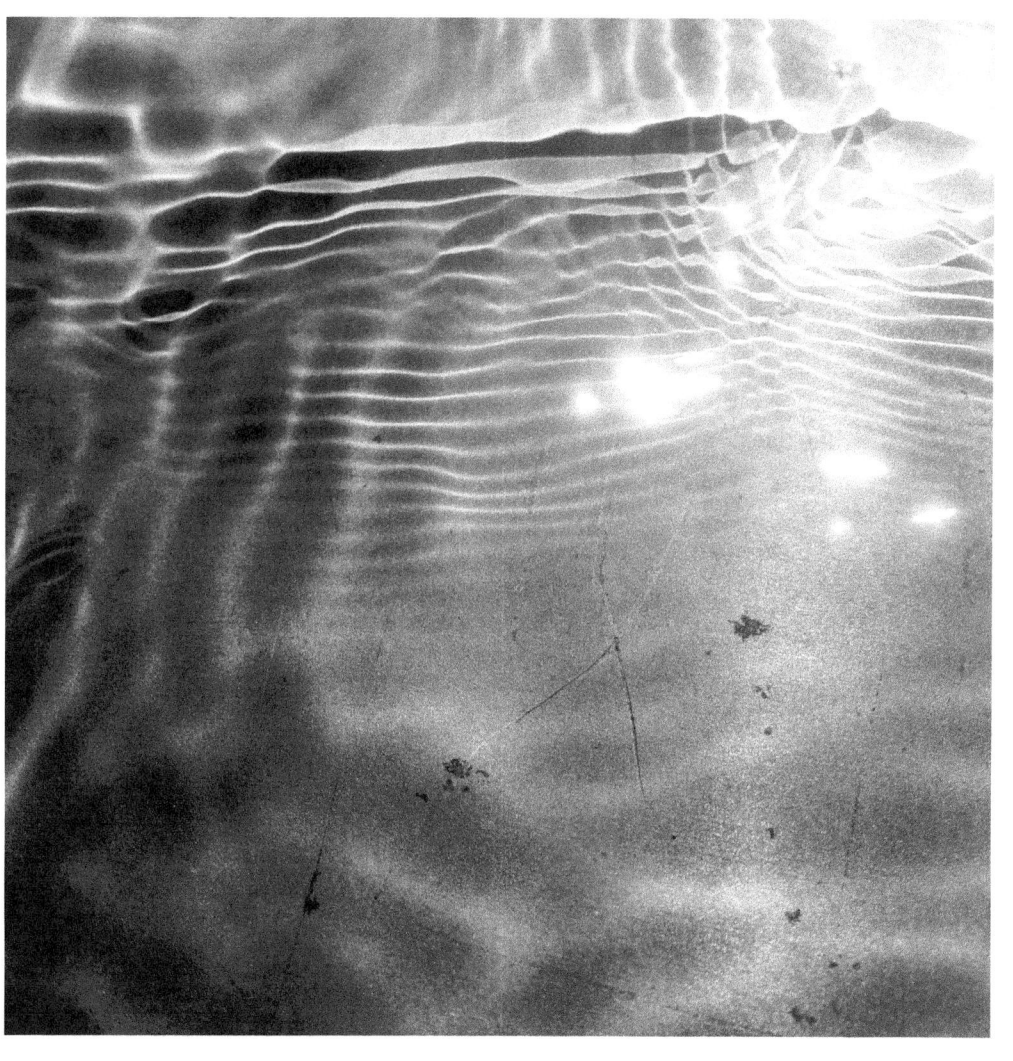

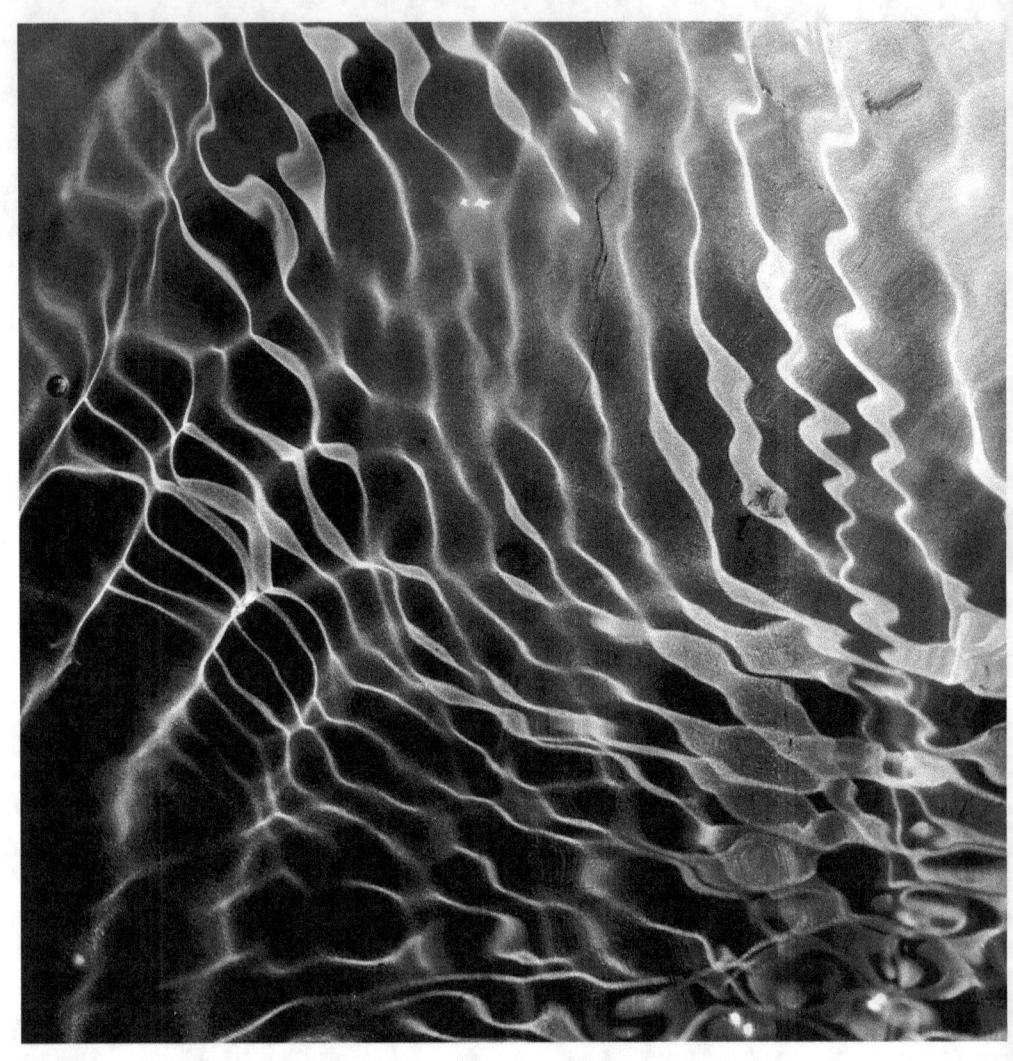

14

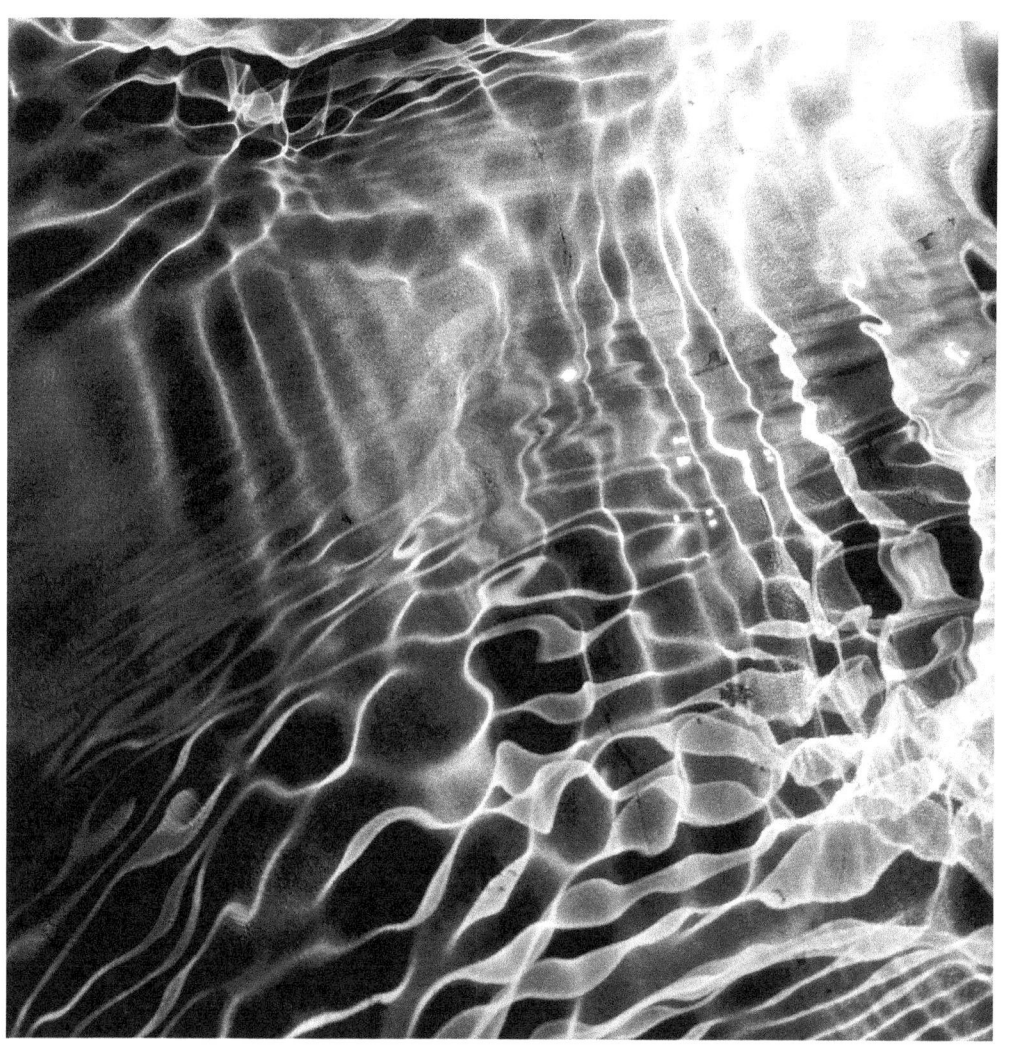

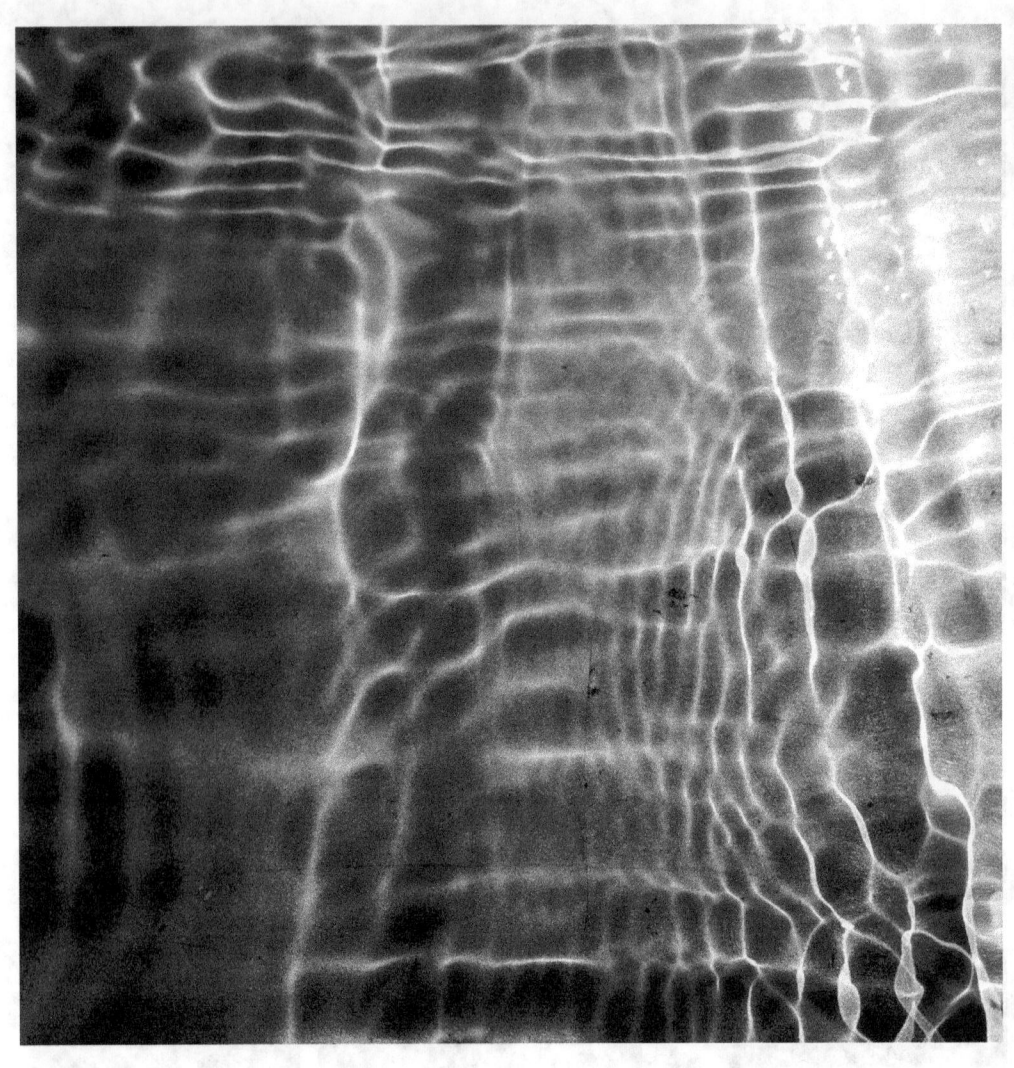

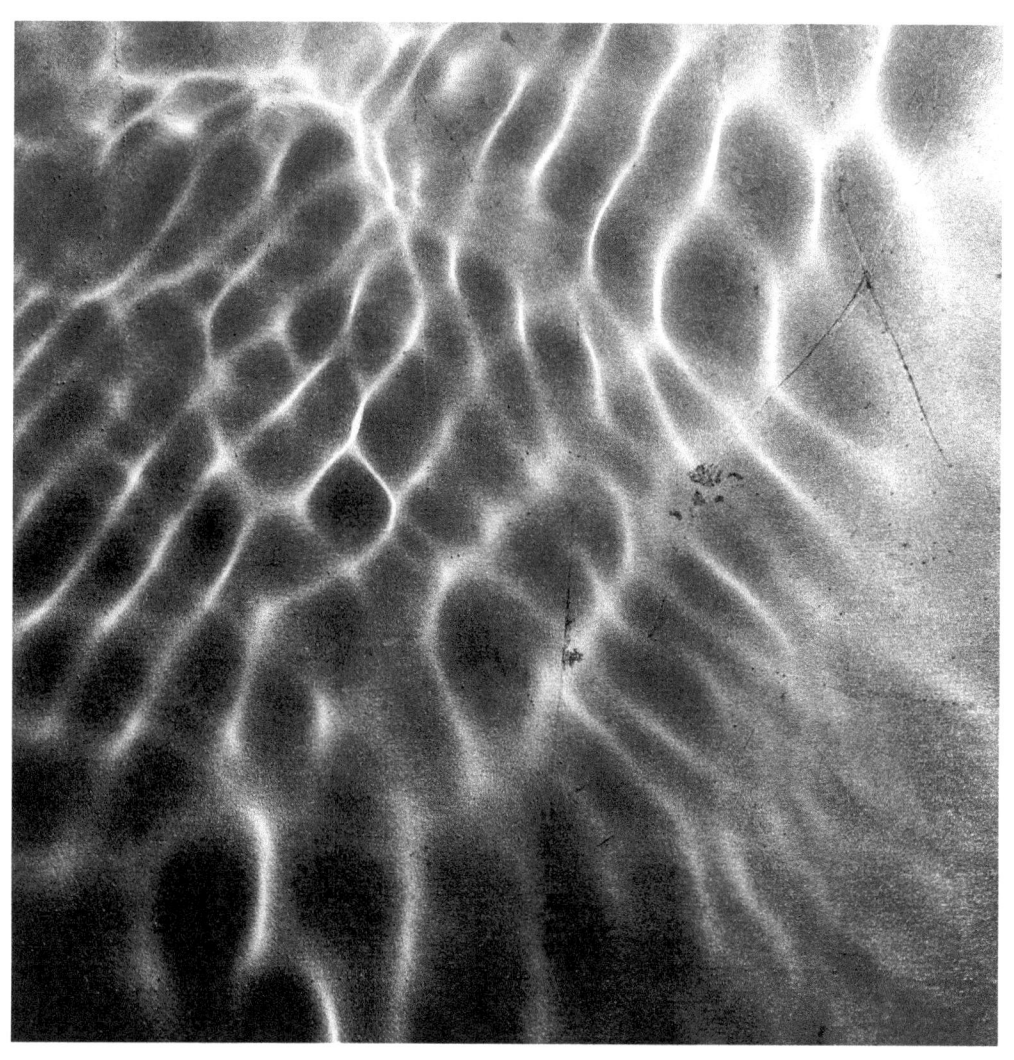

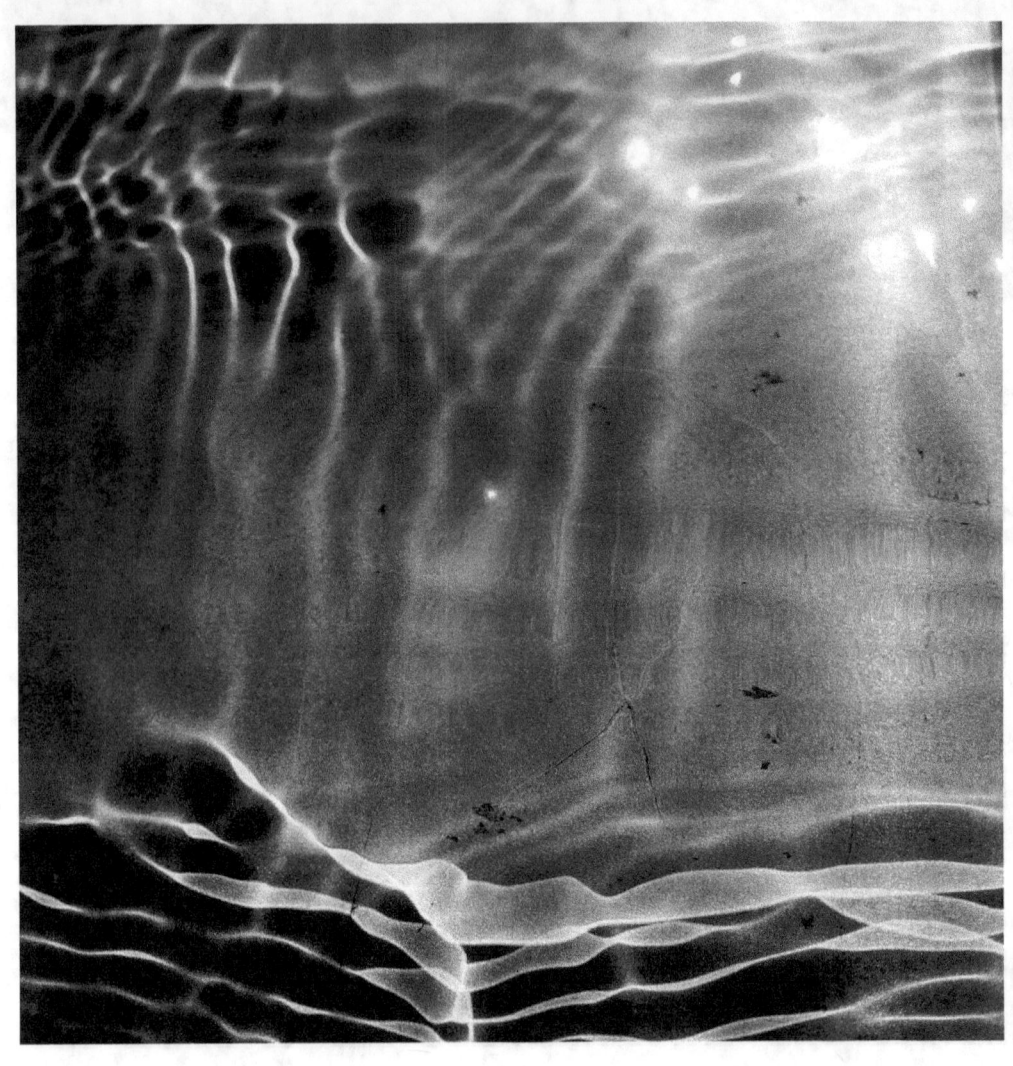

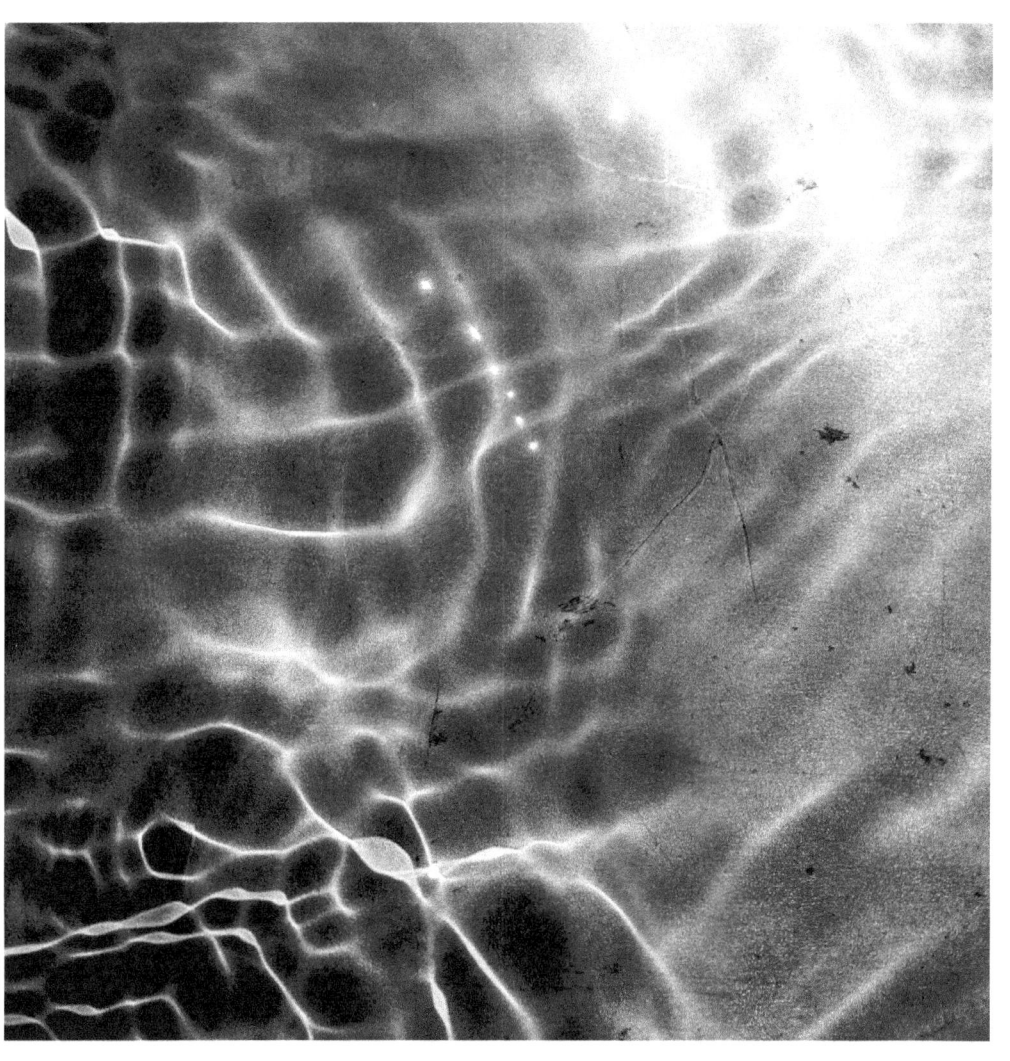

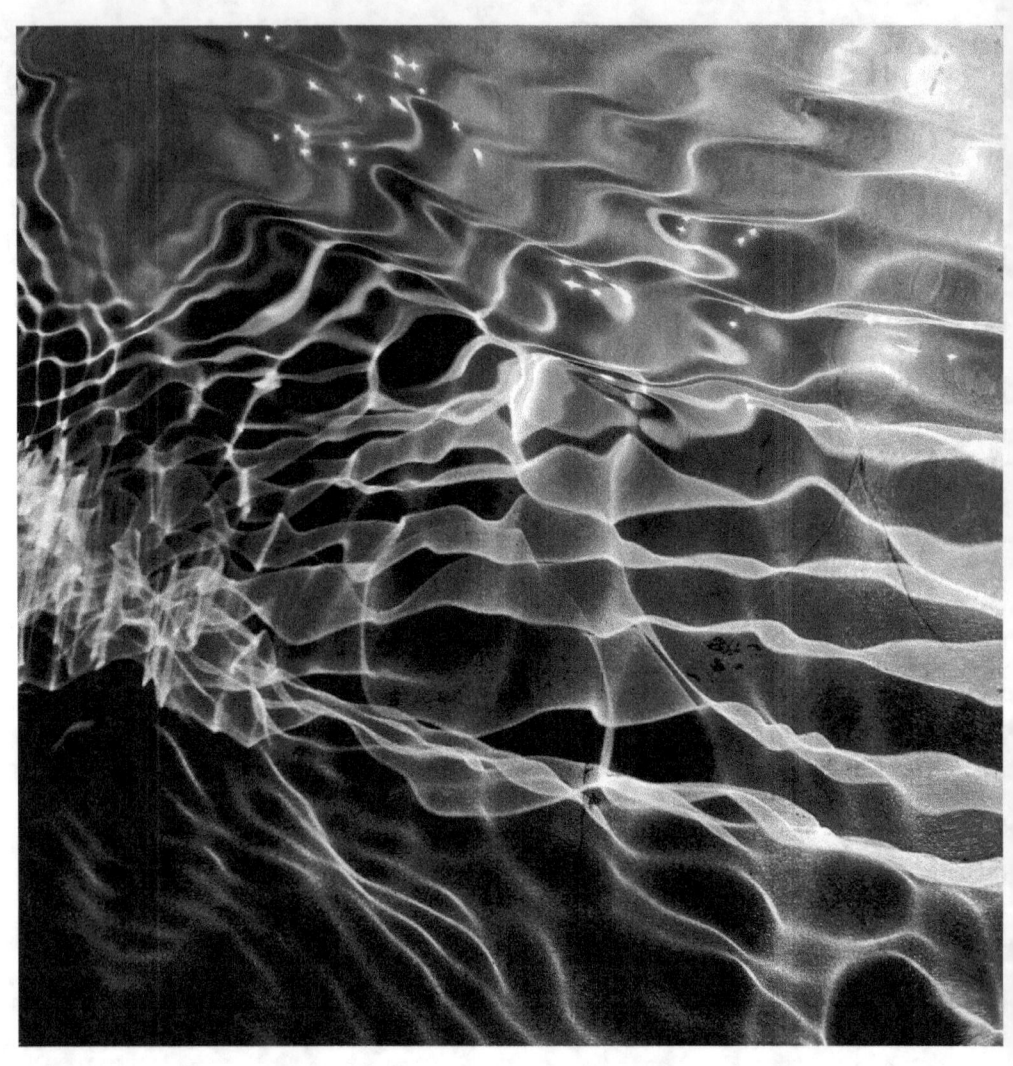

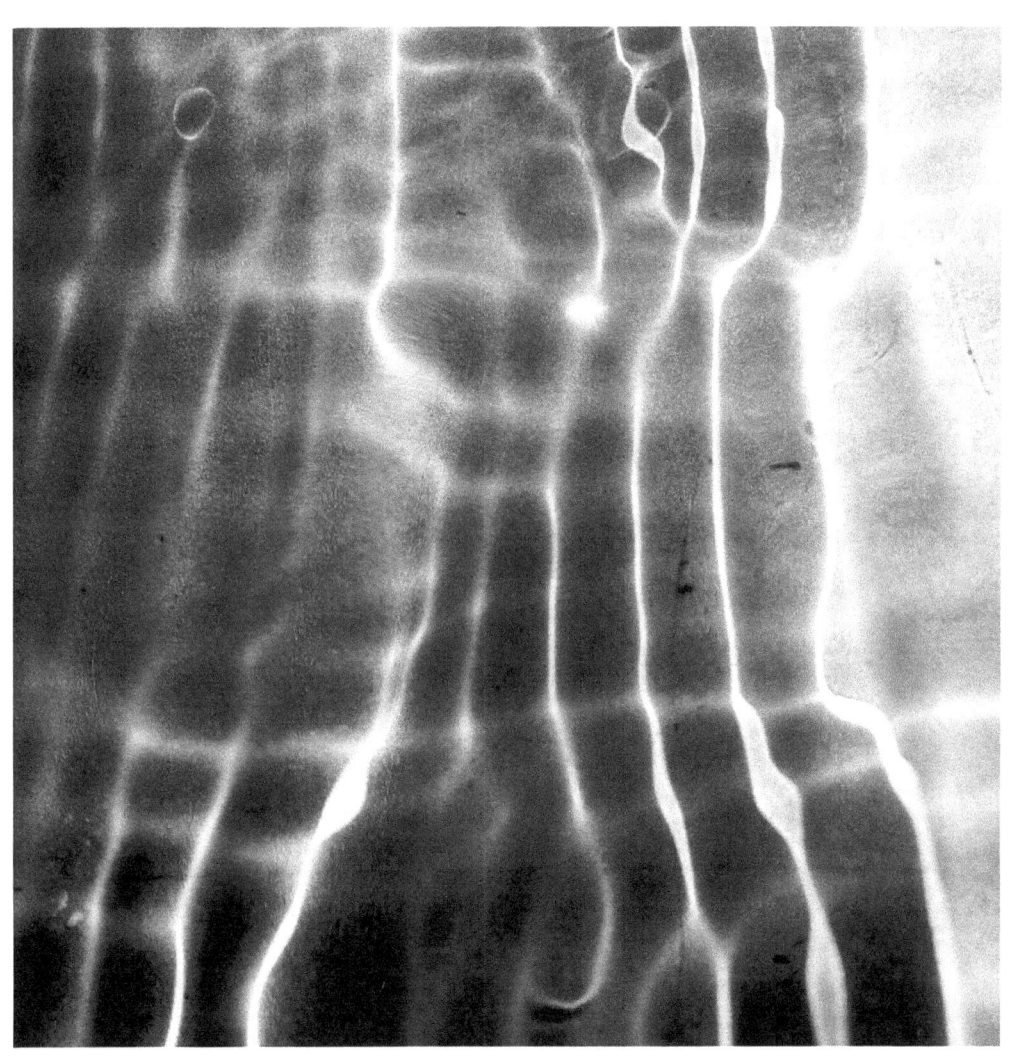

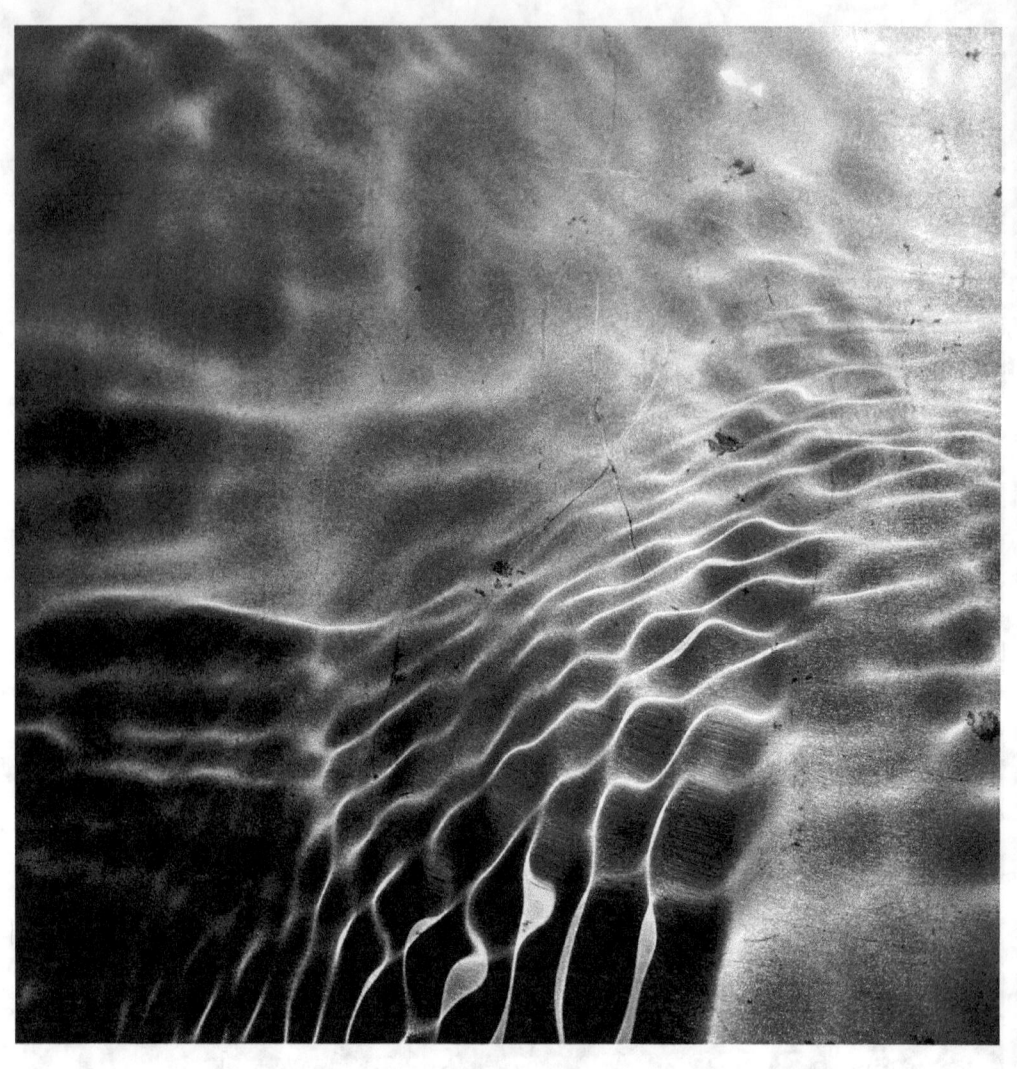

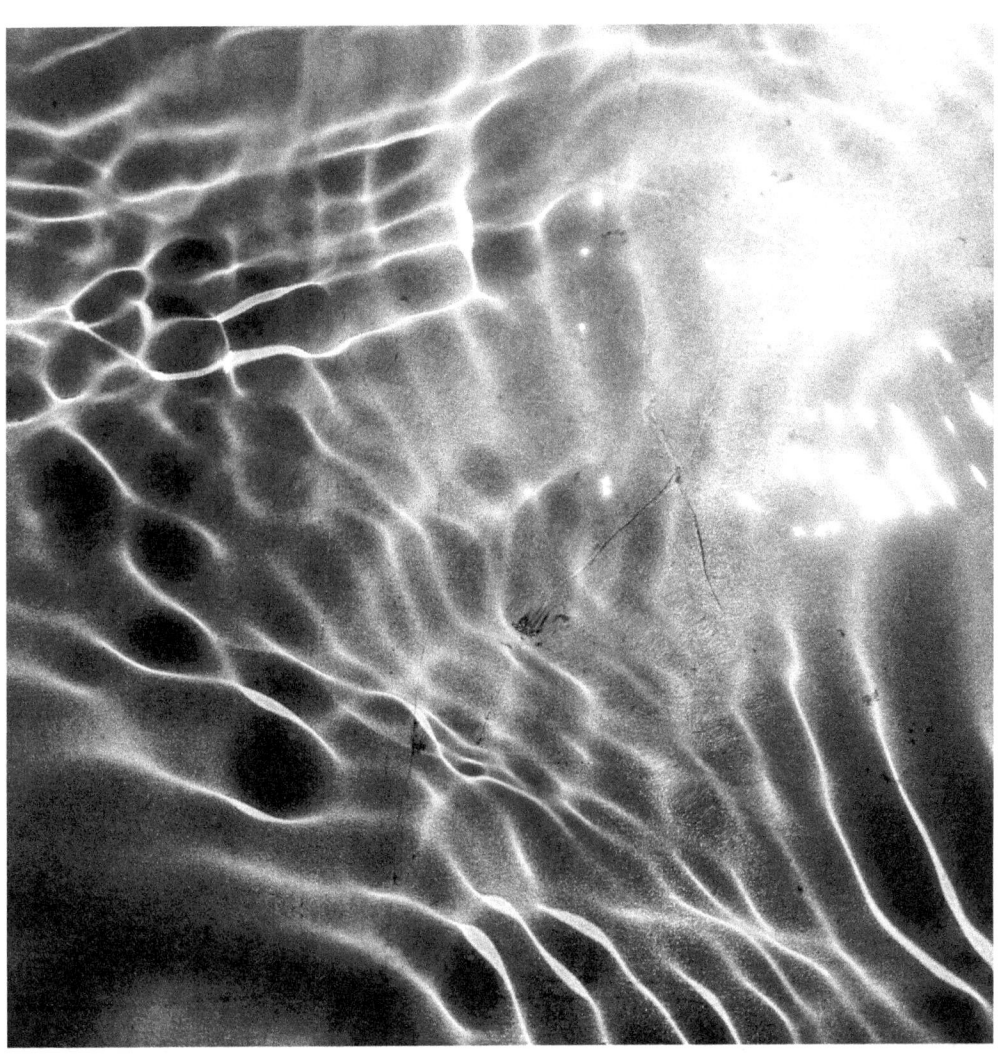

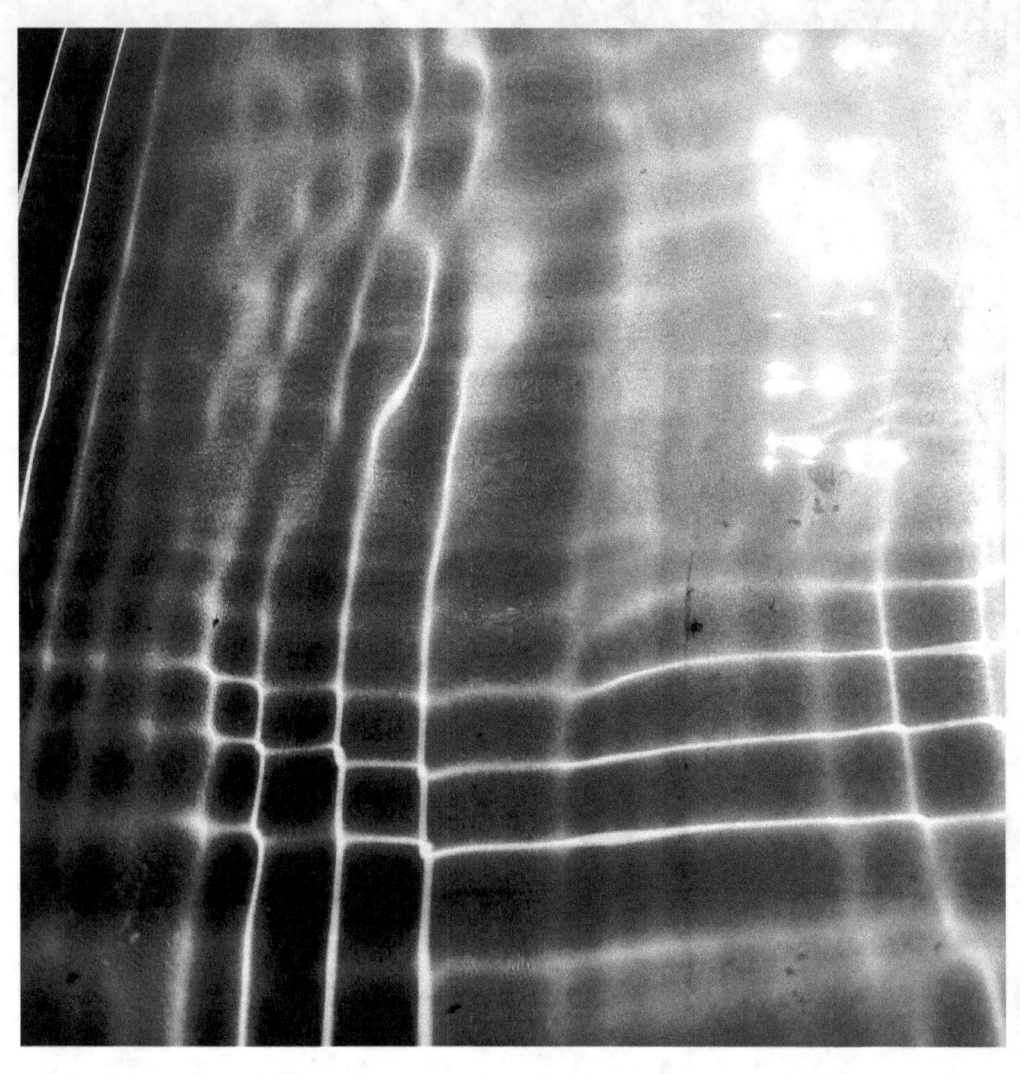

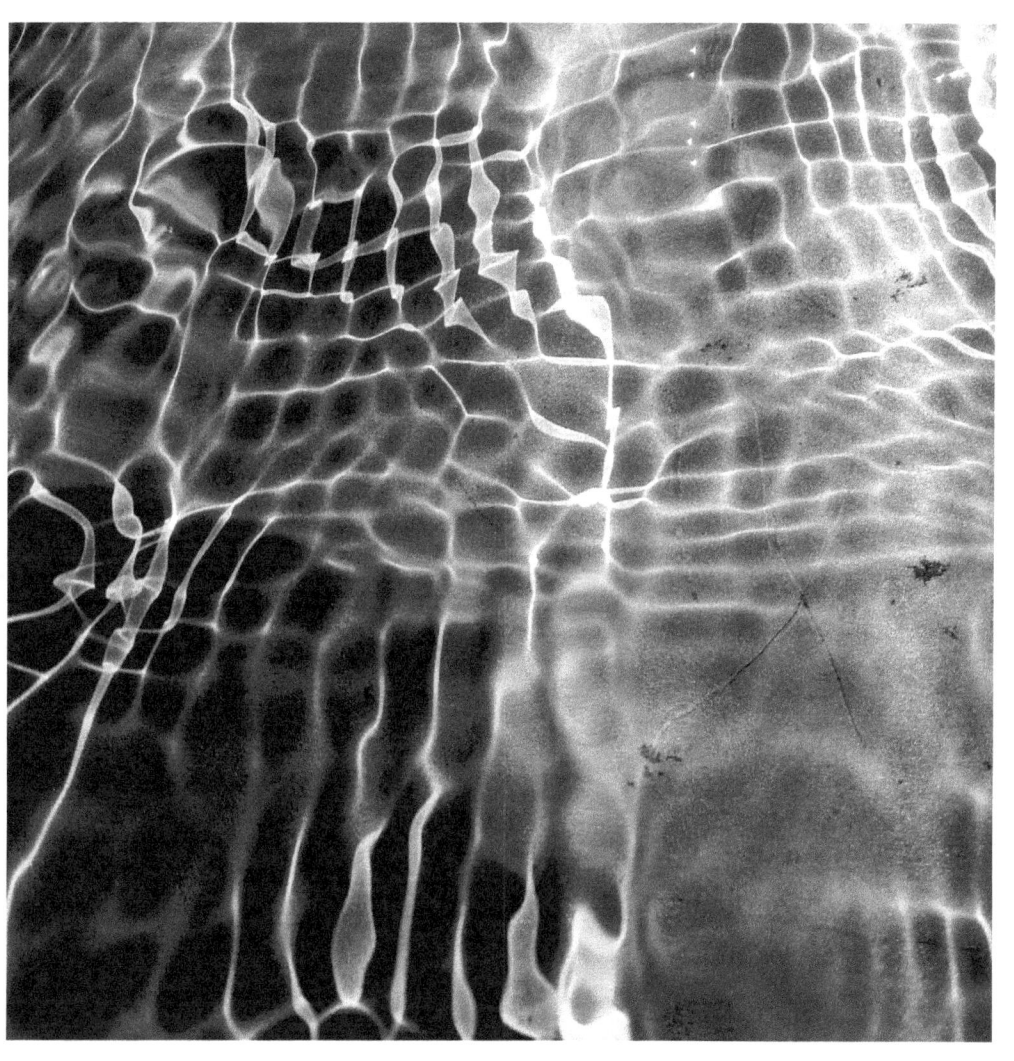

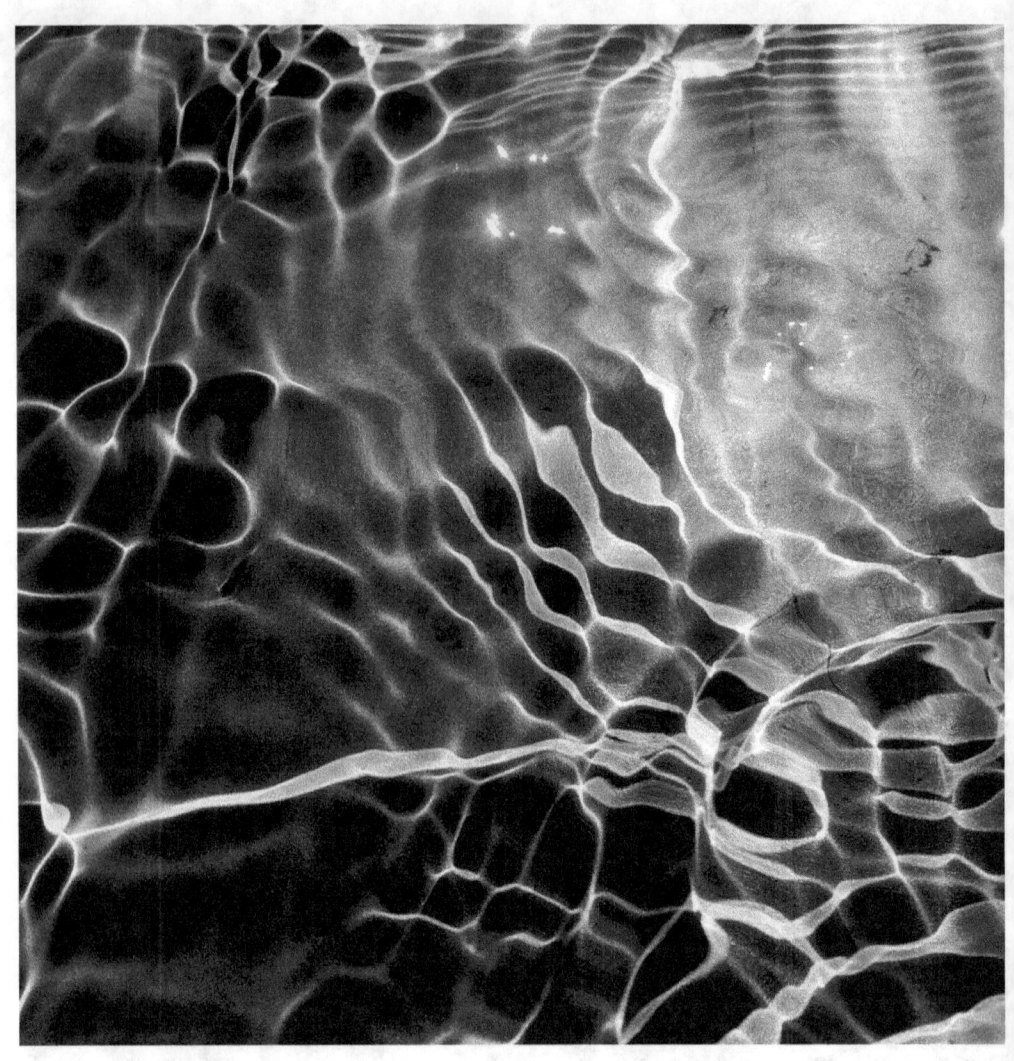

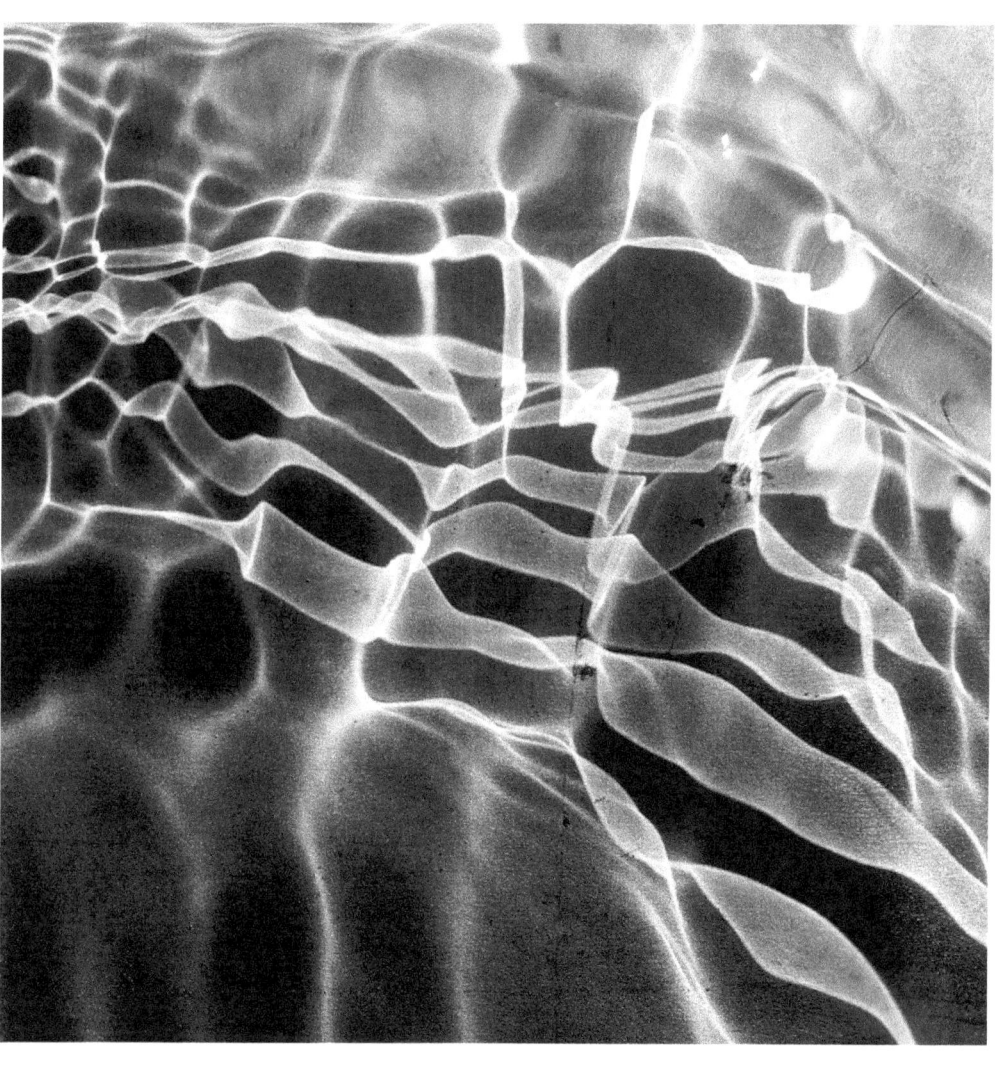

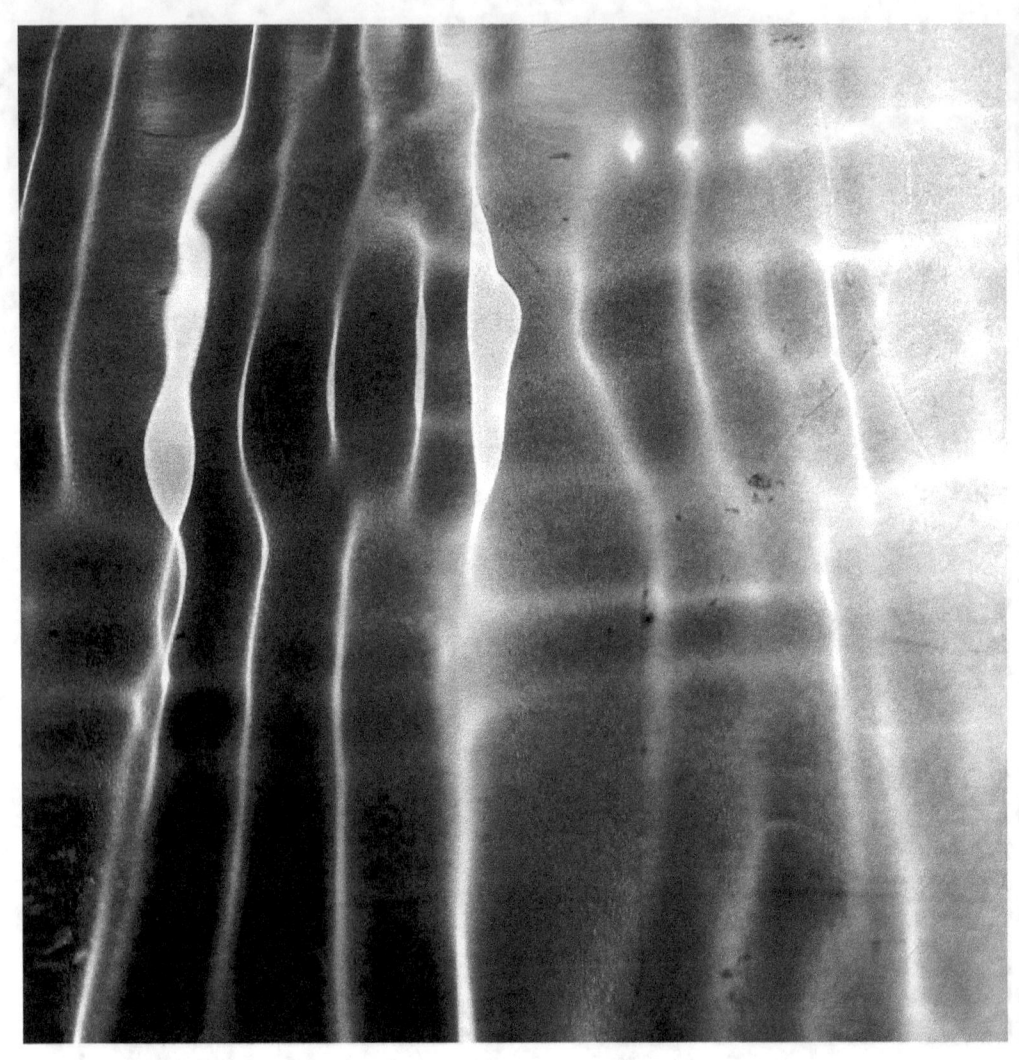

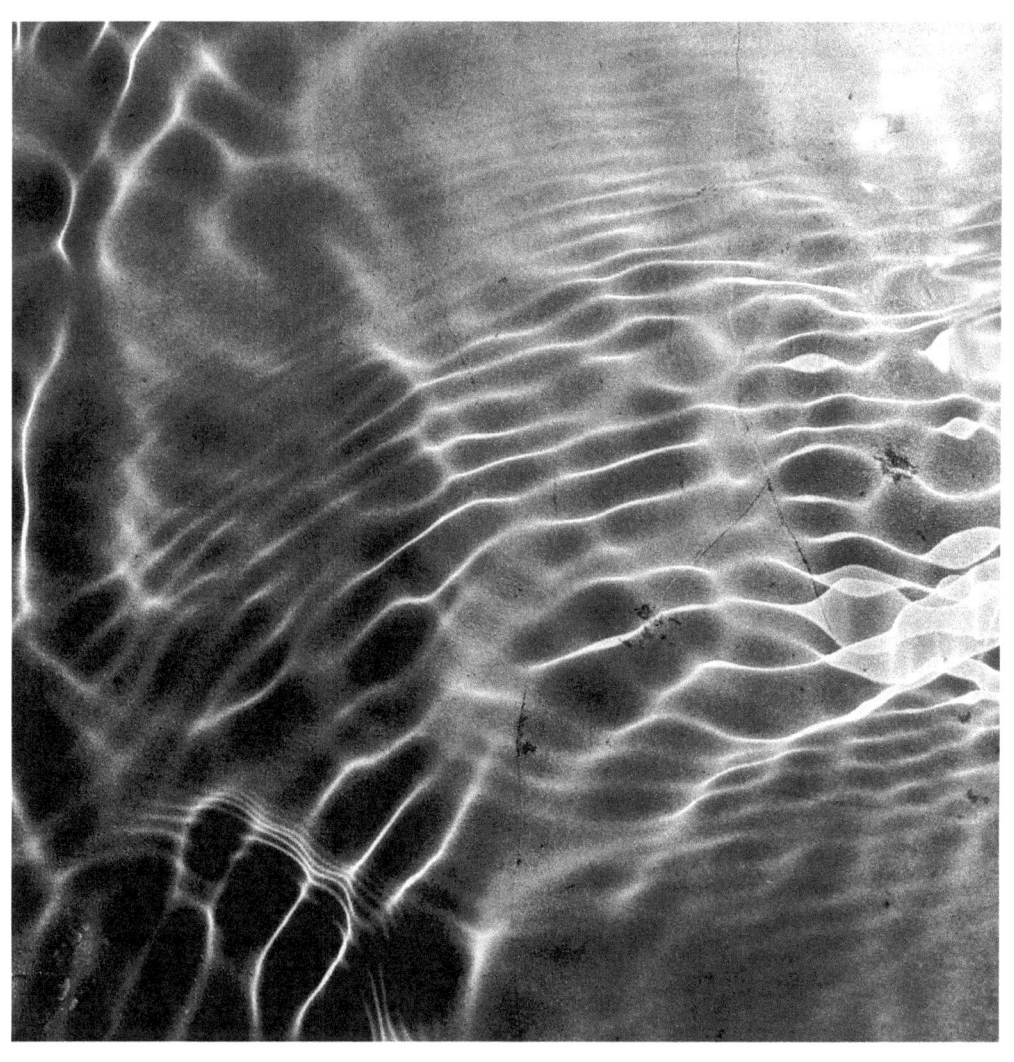

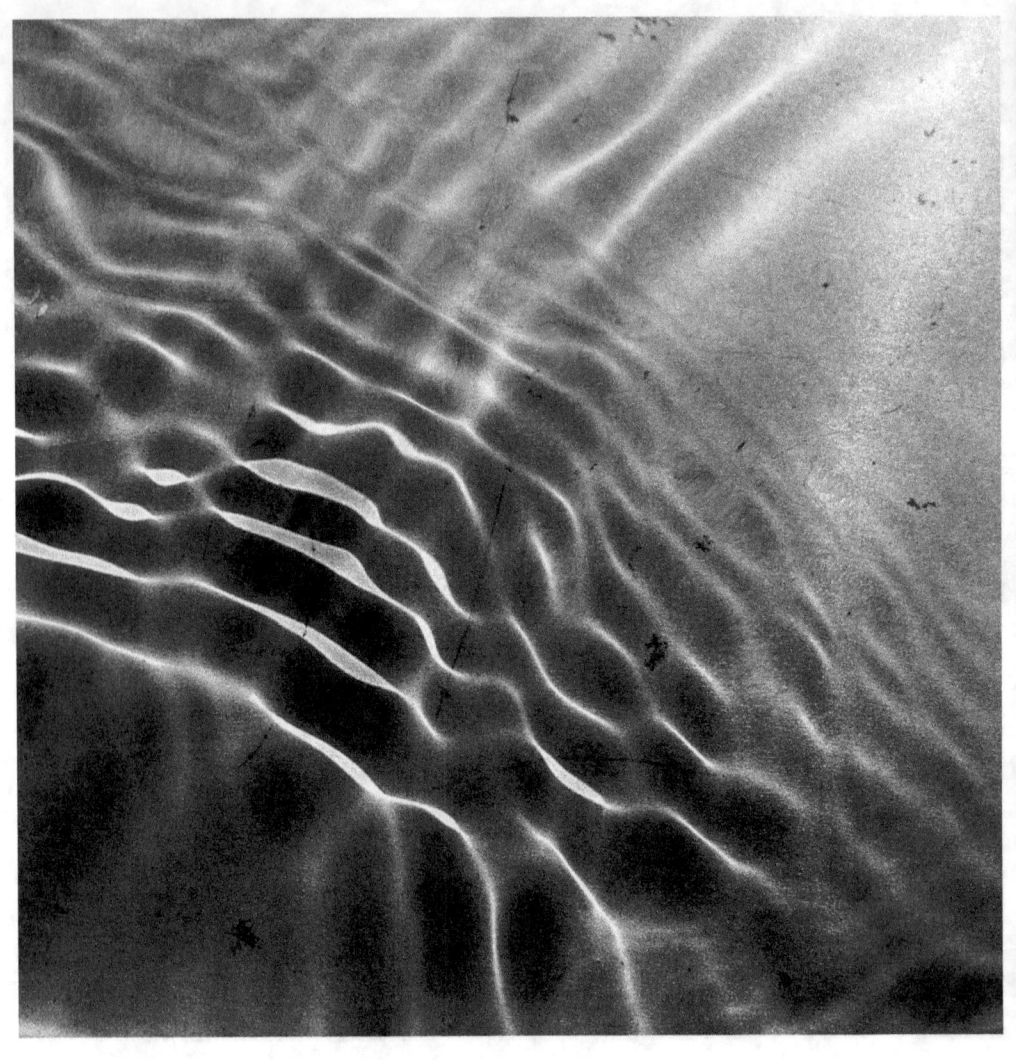

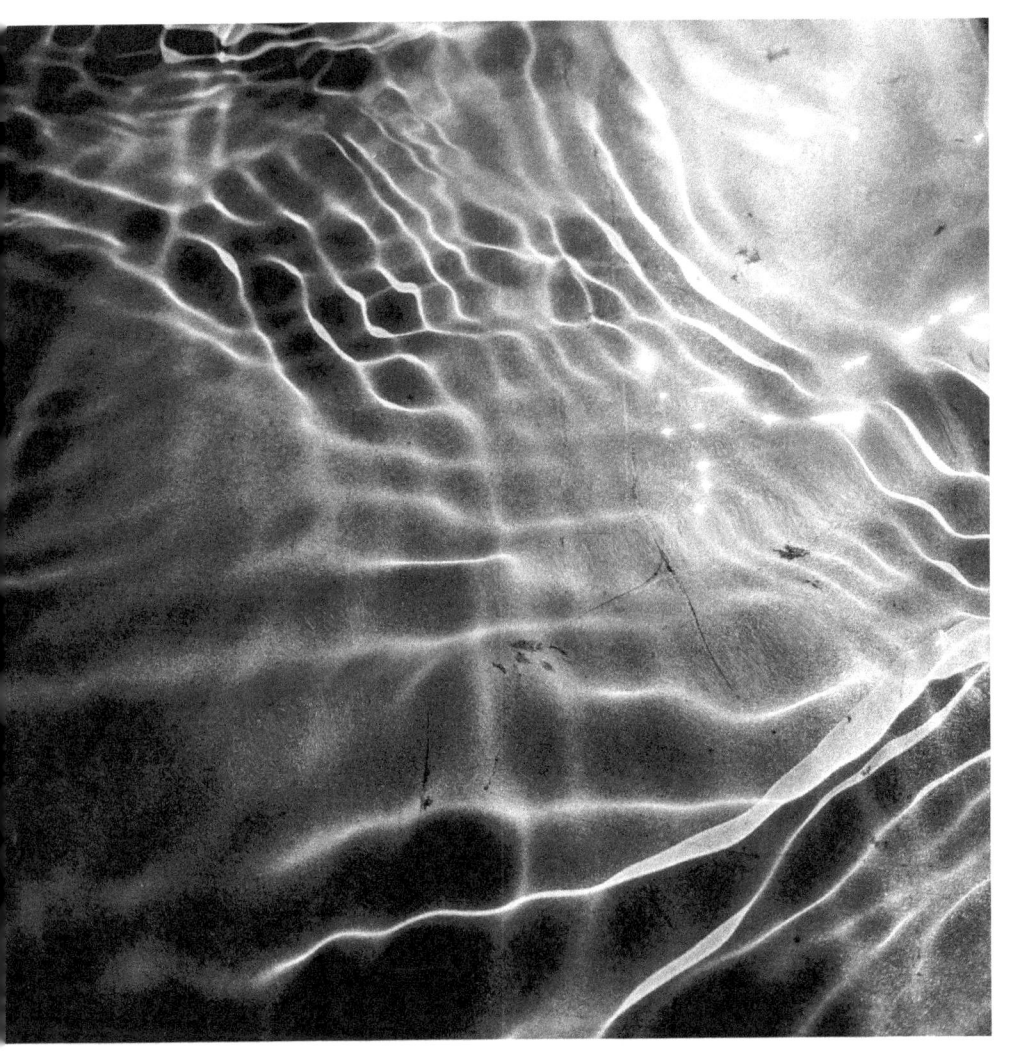

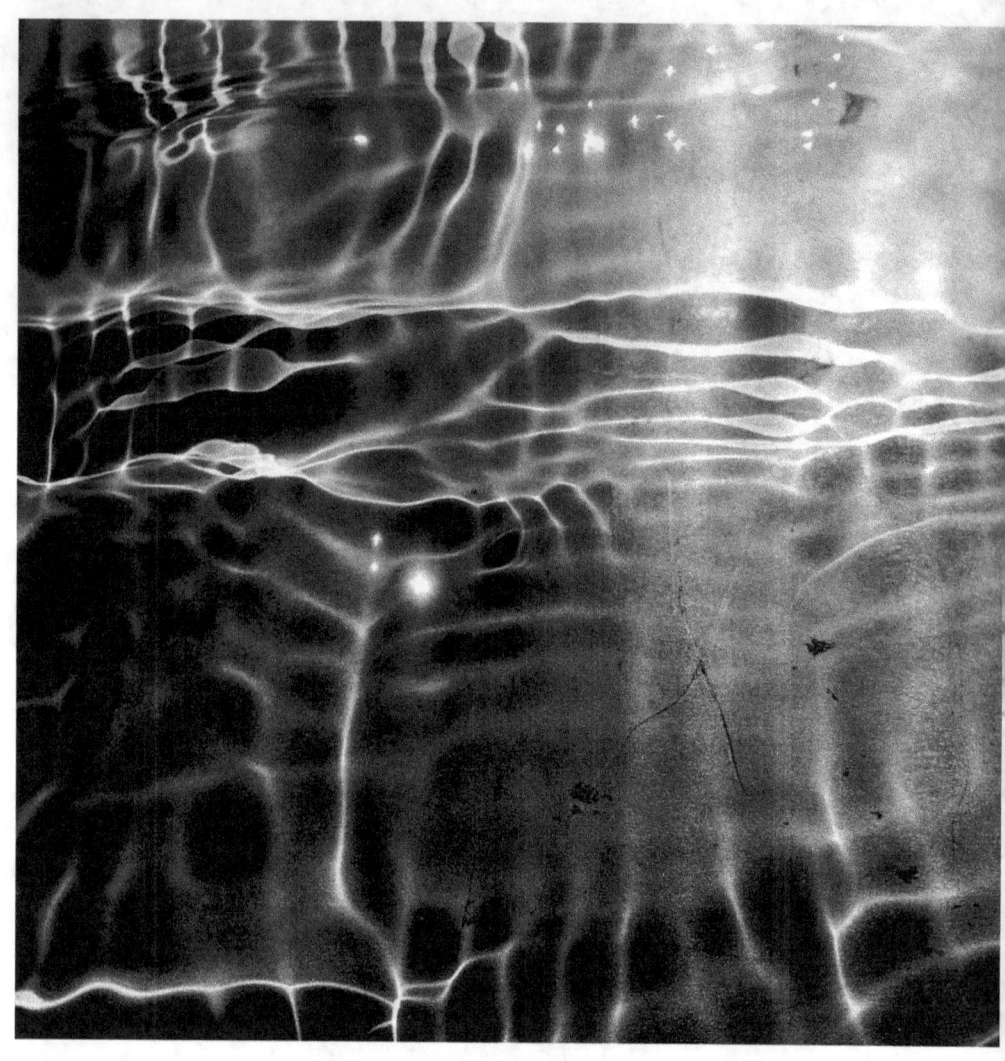

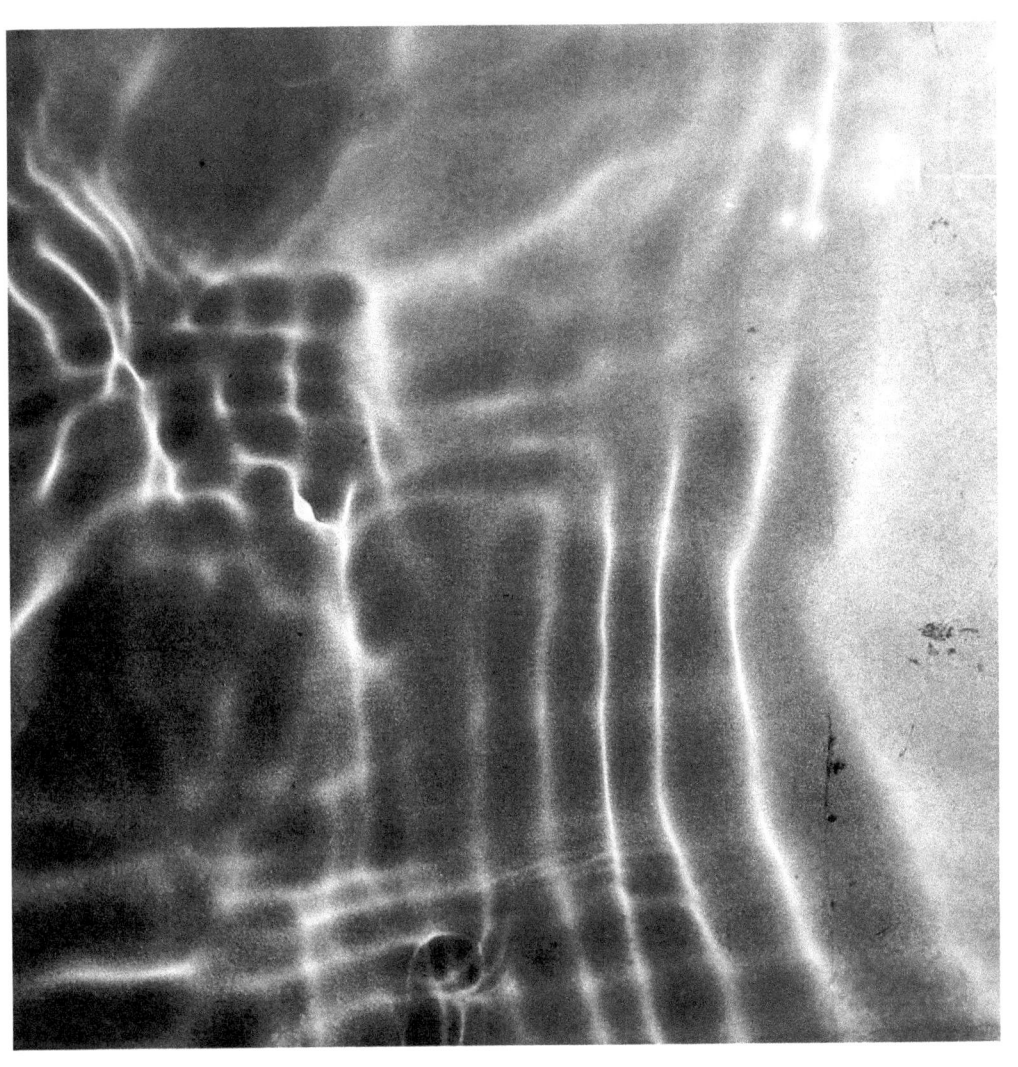

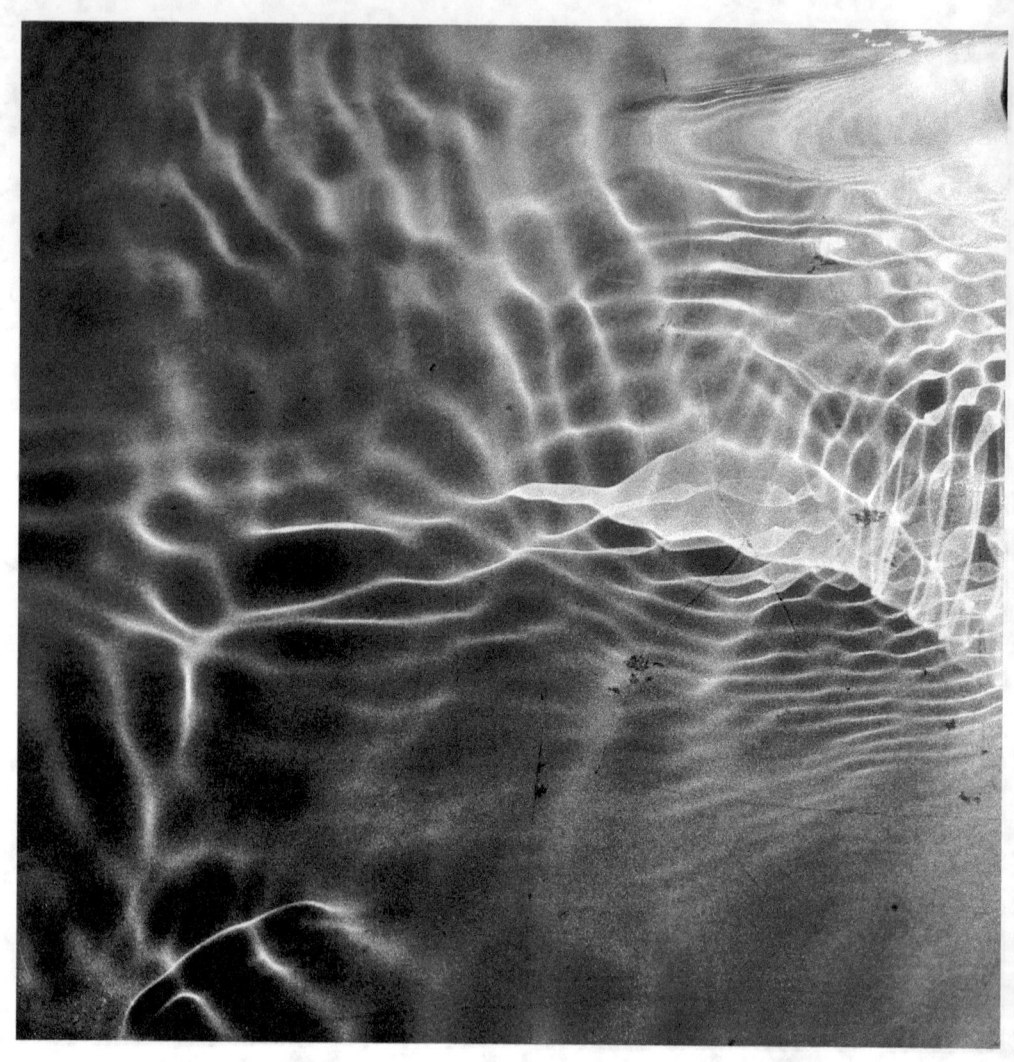

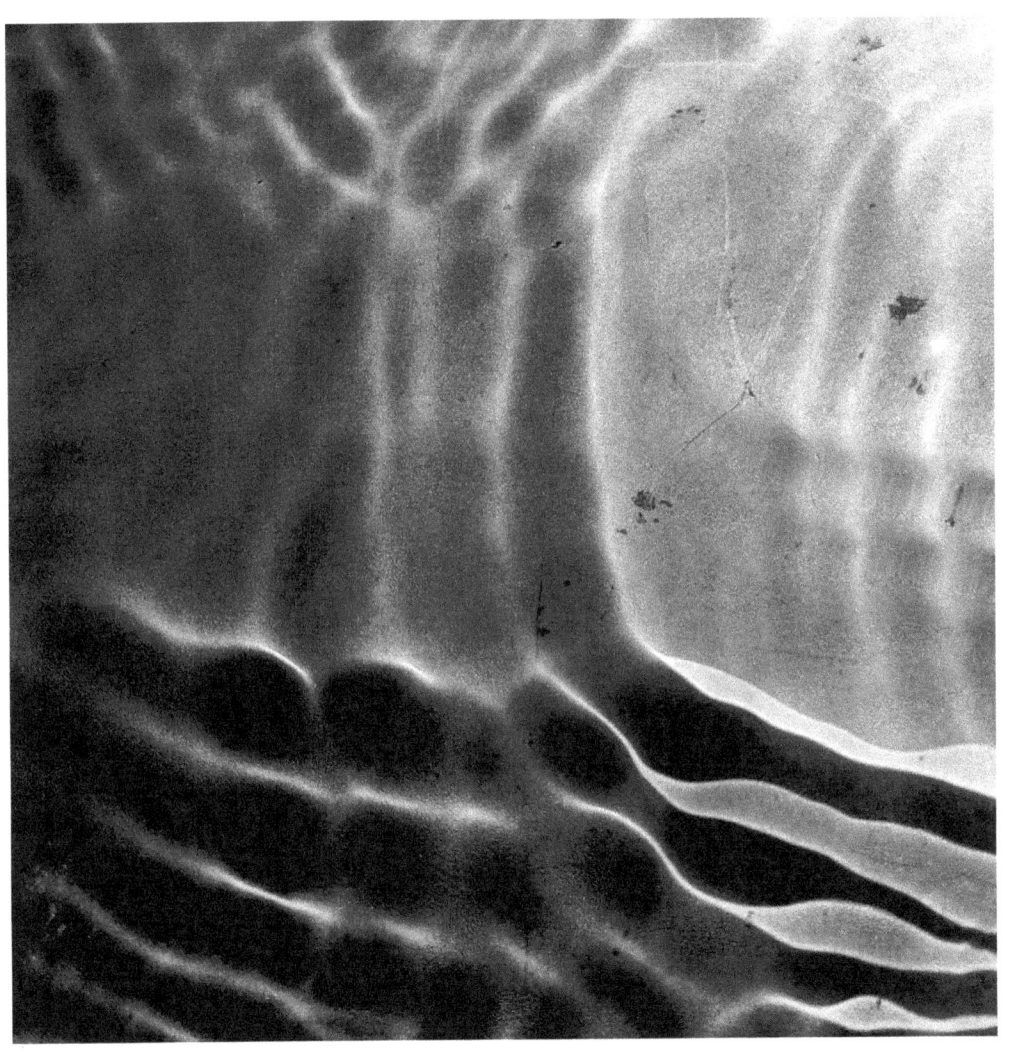

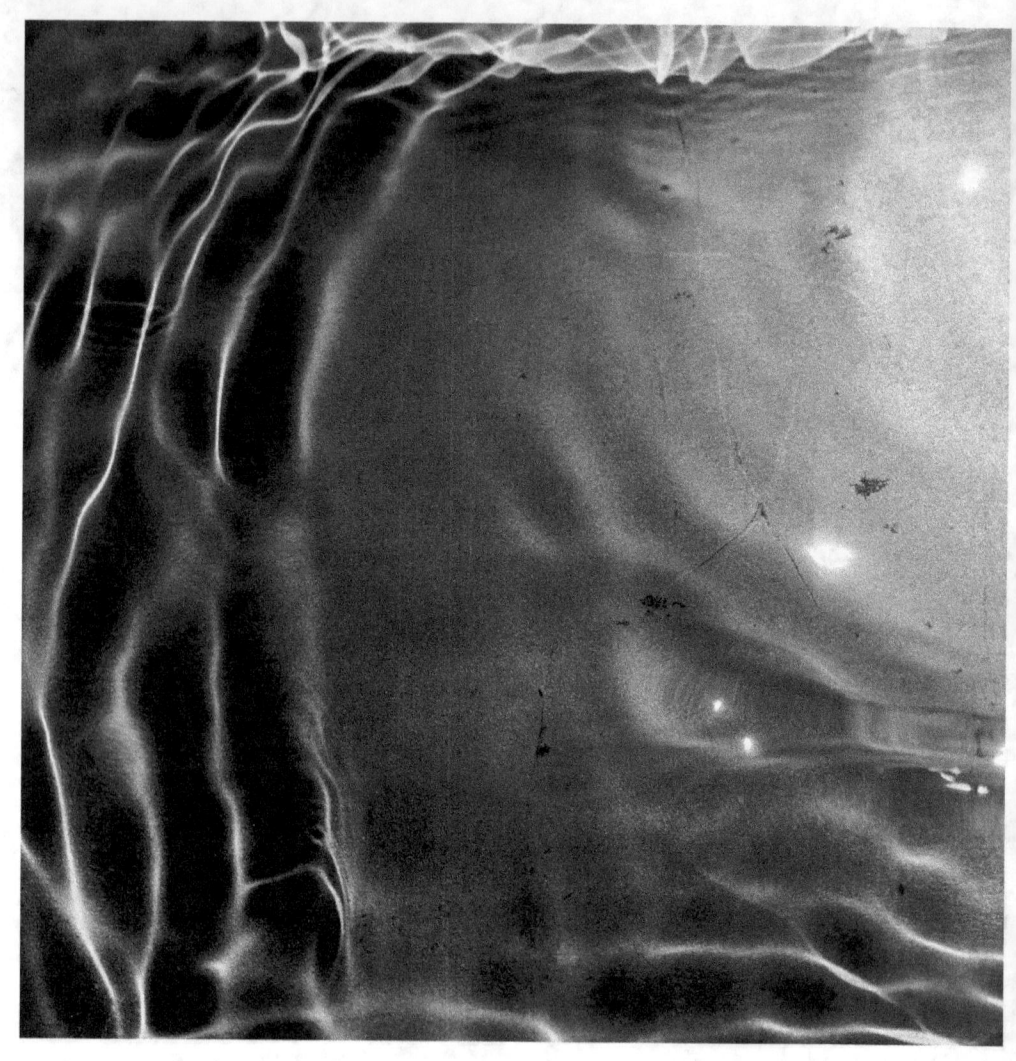

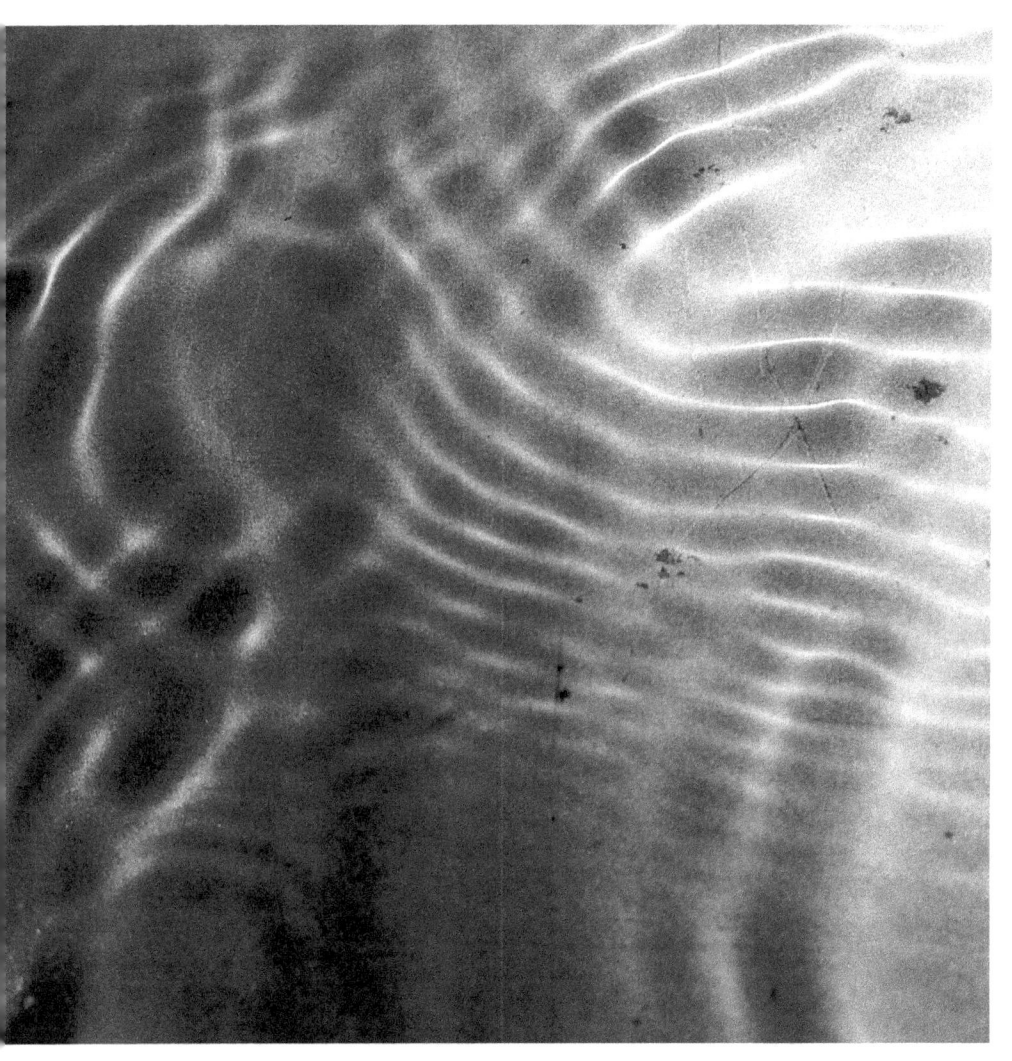

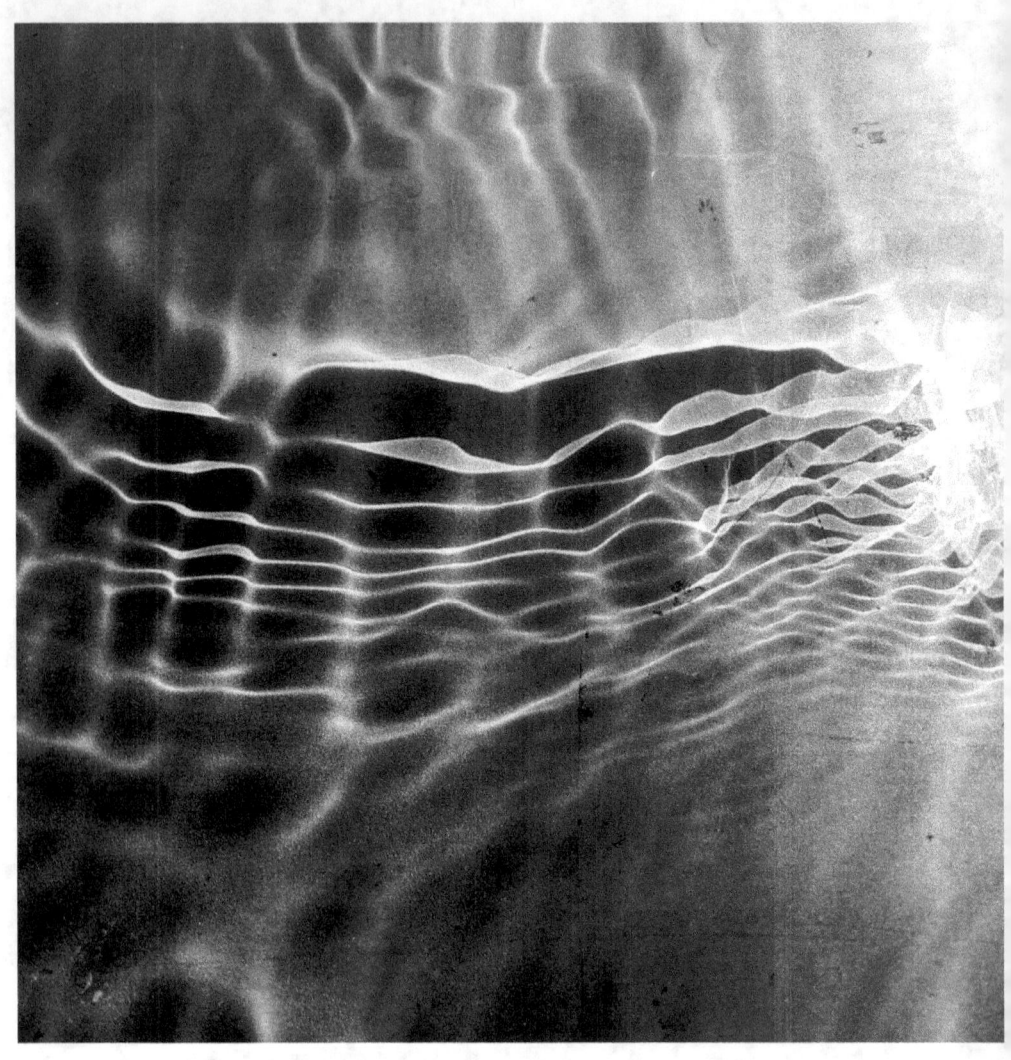

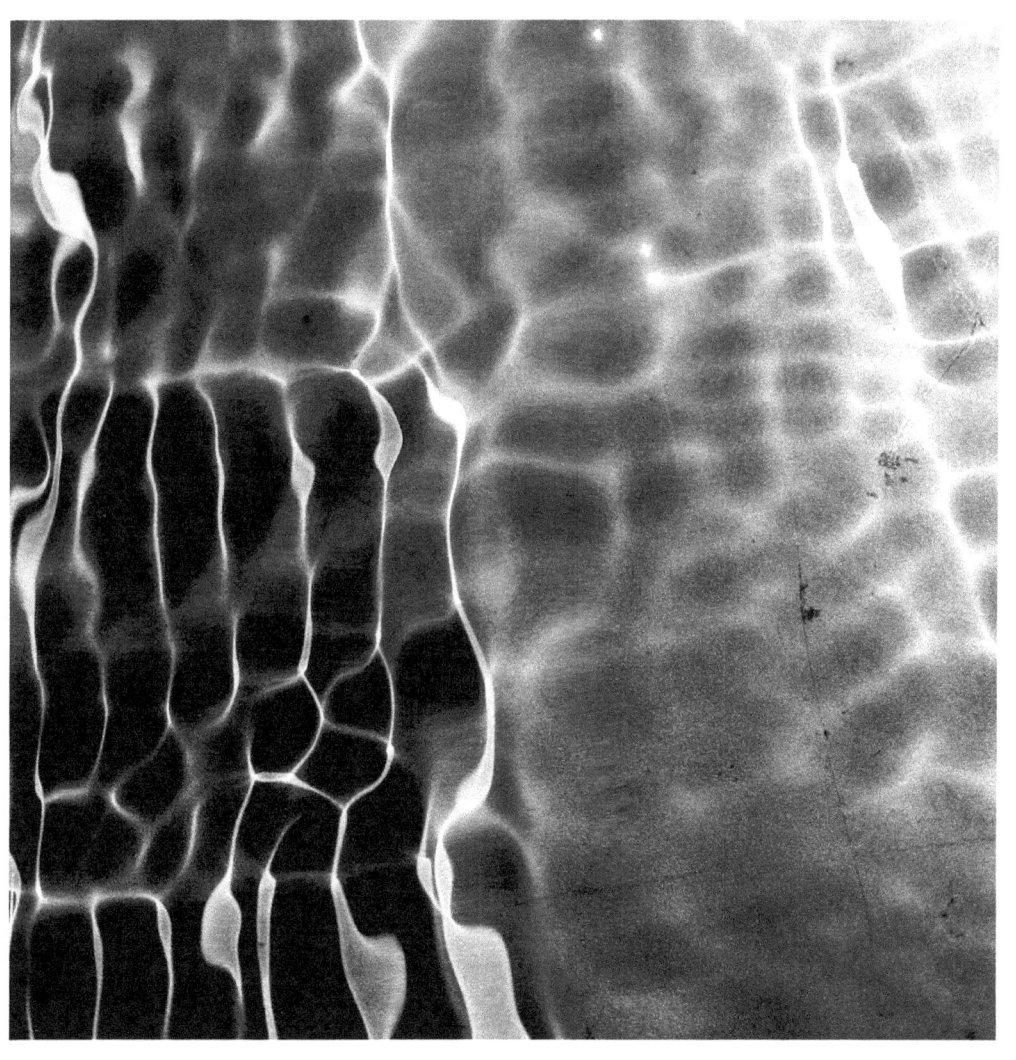

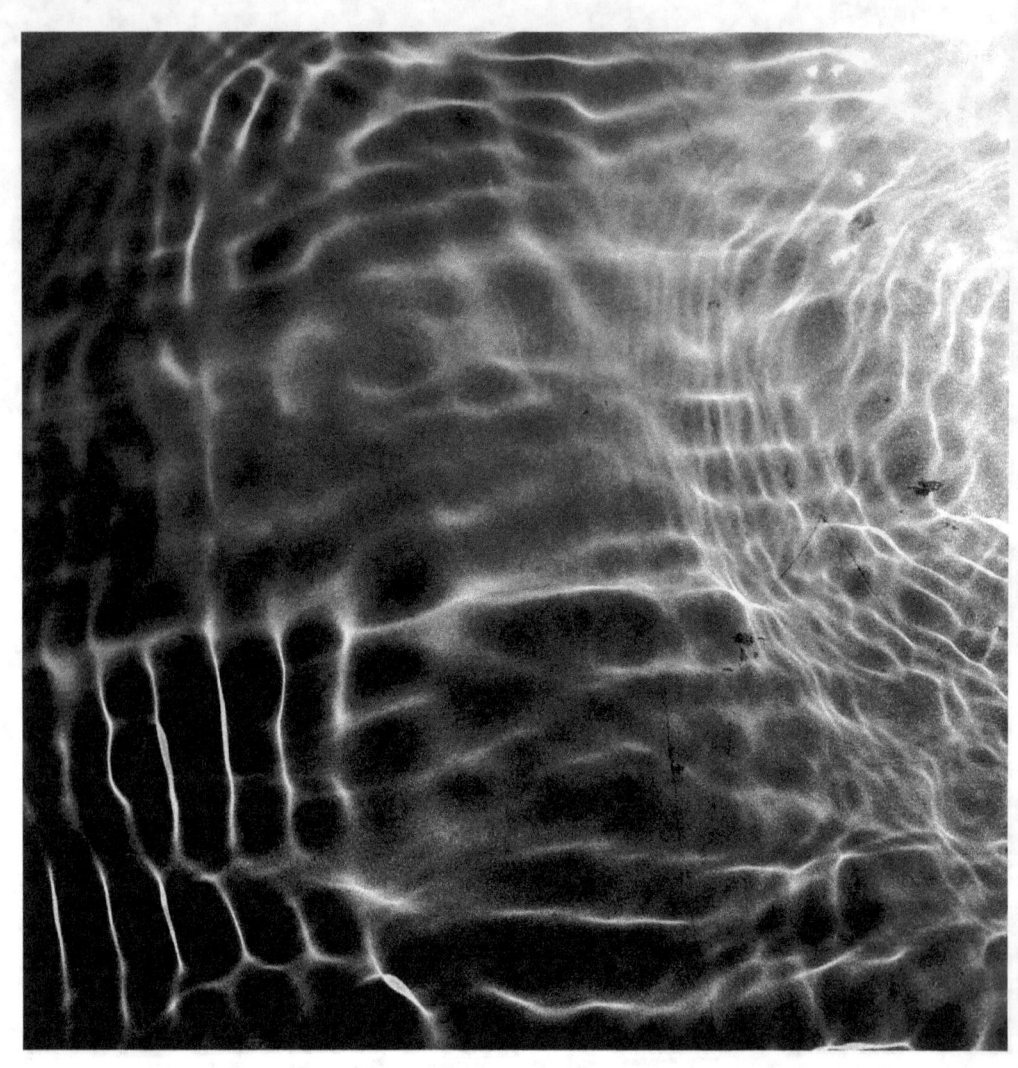

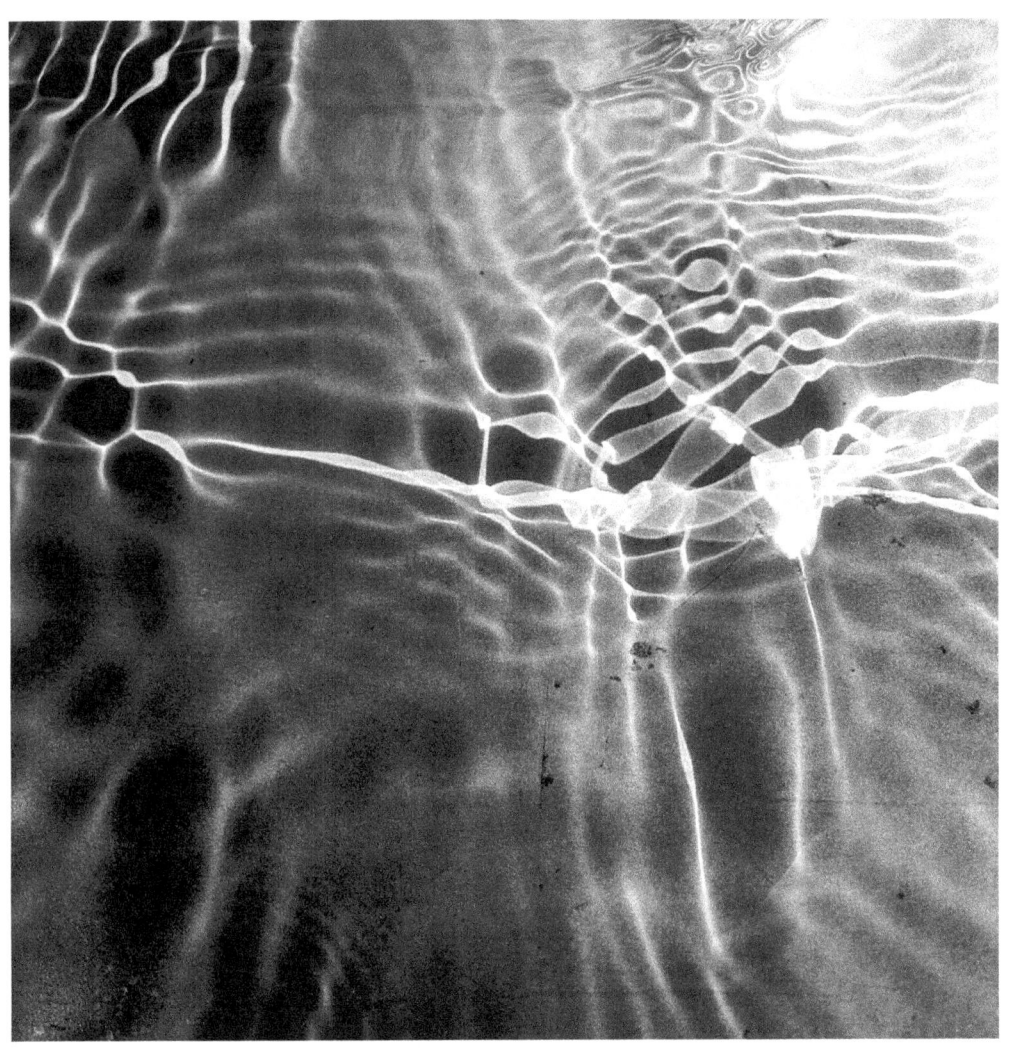

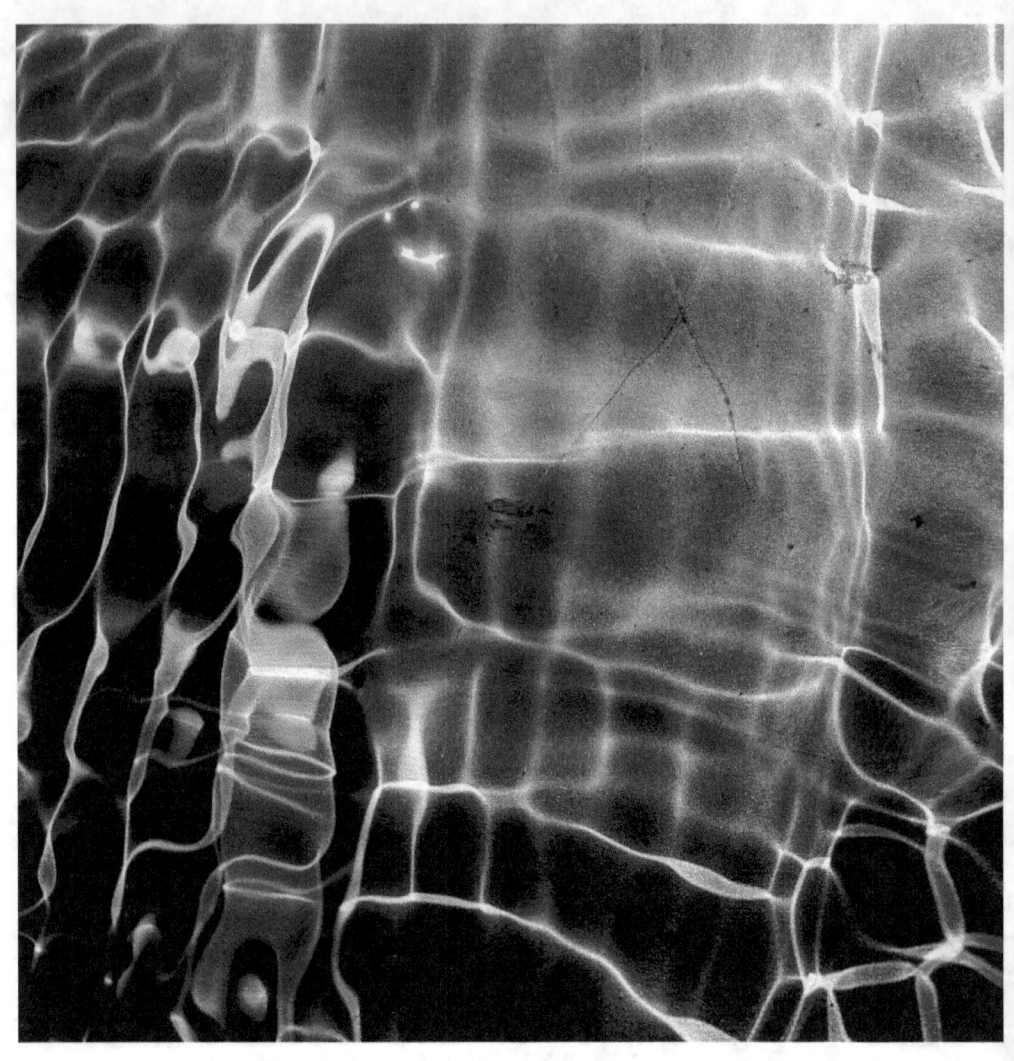

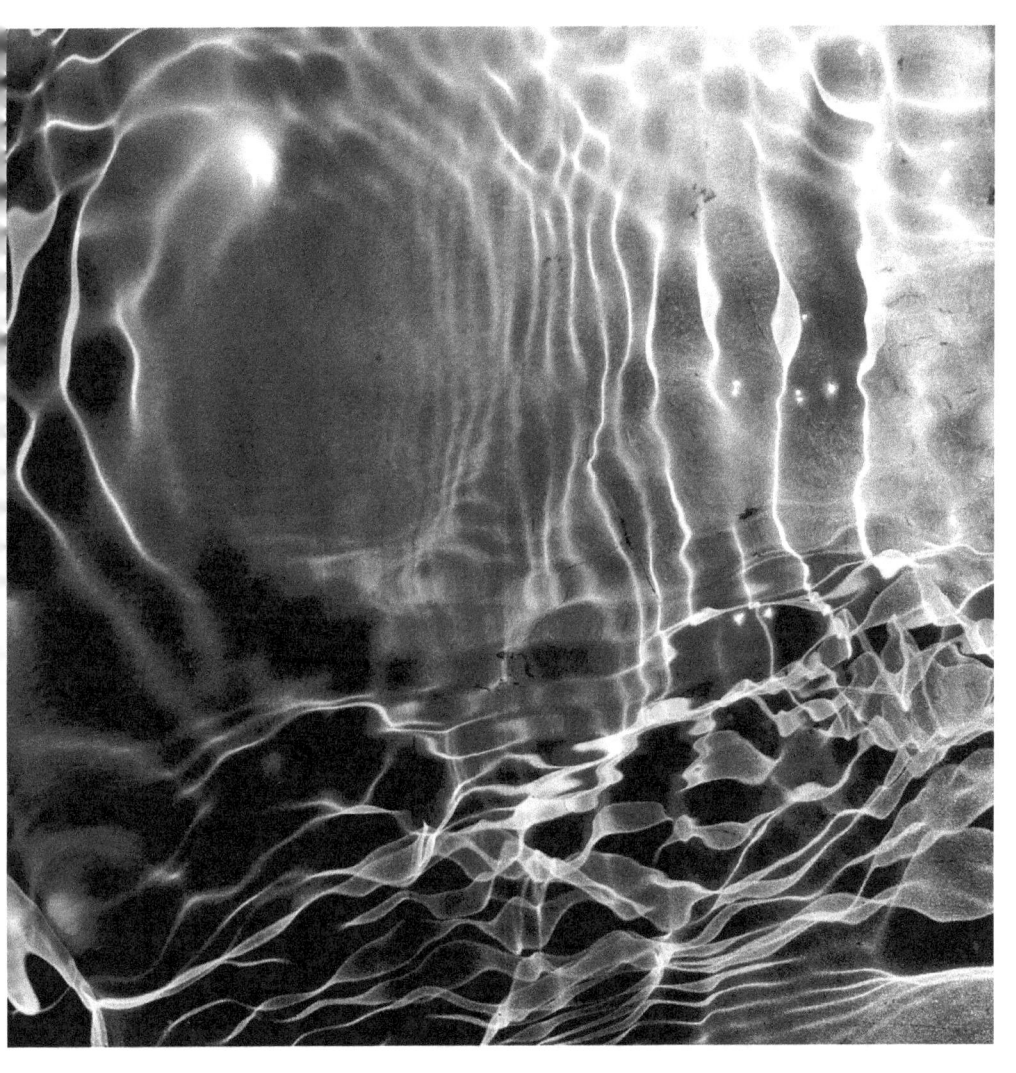

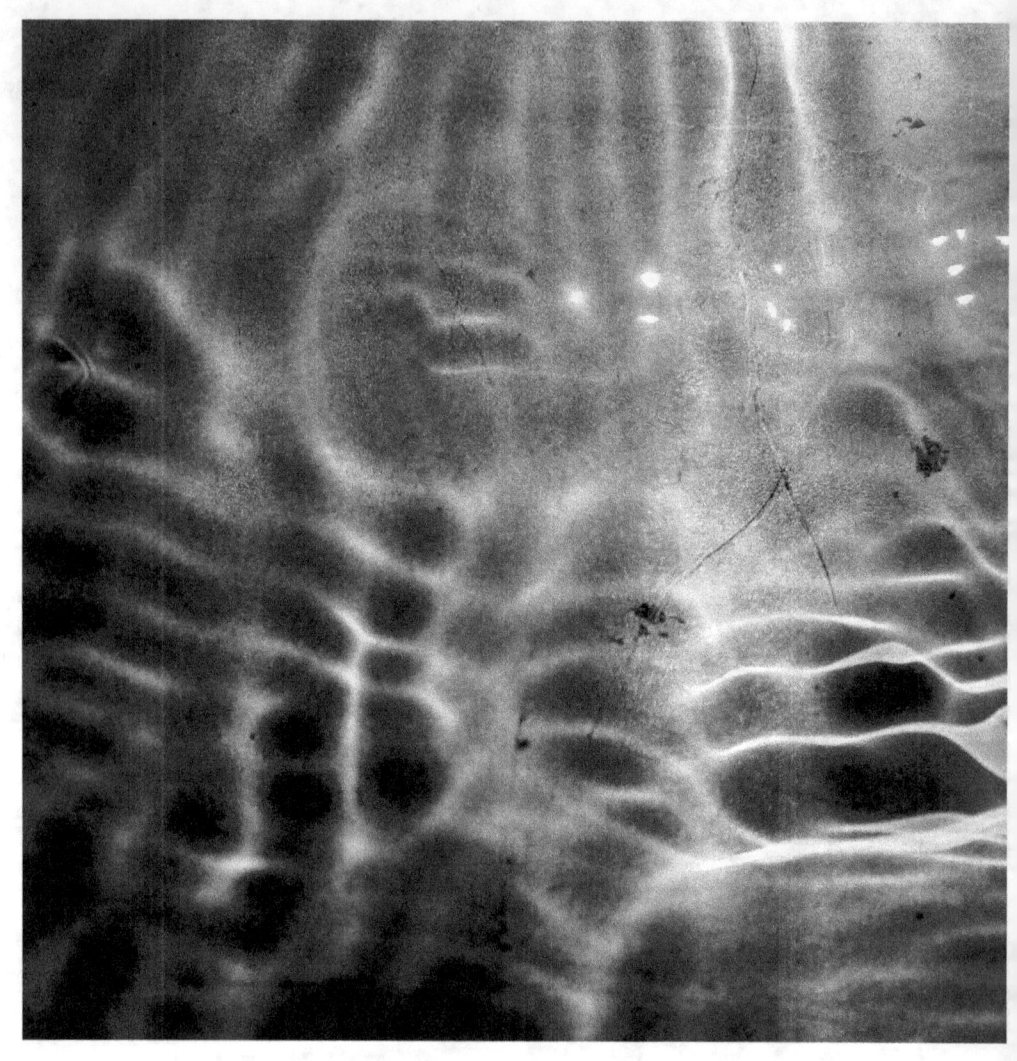

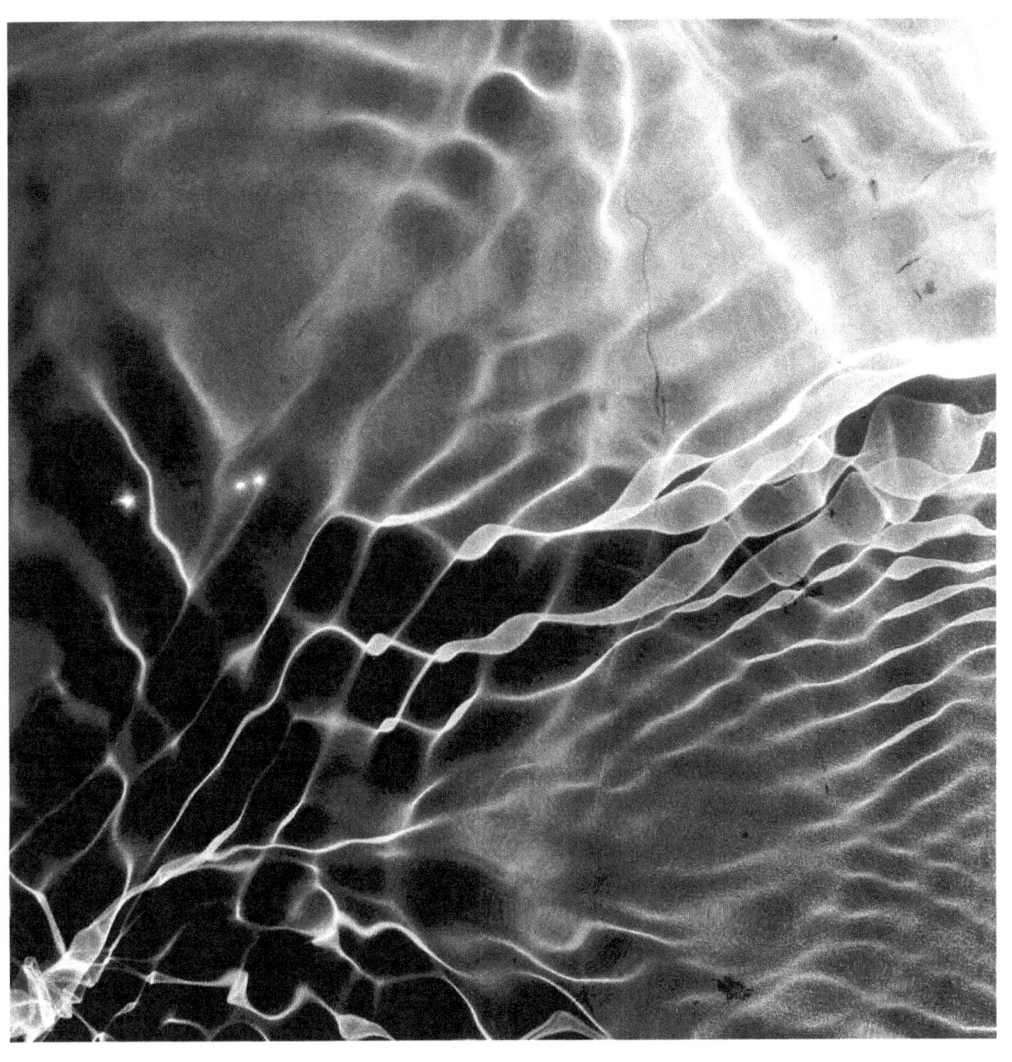

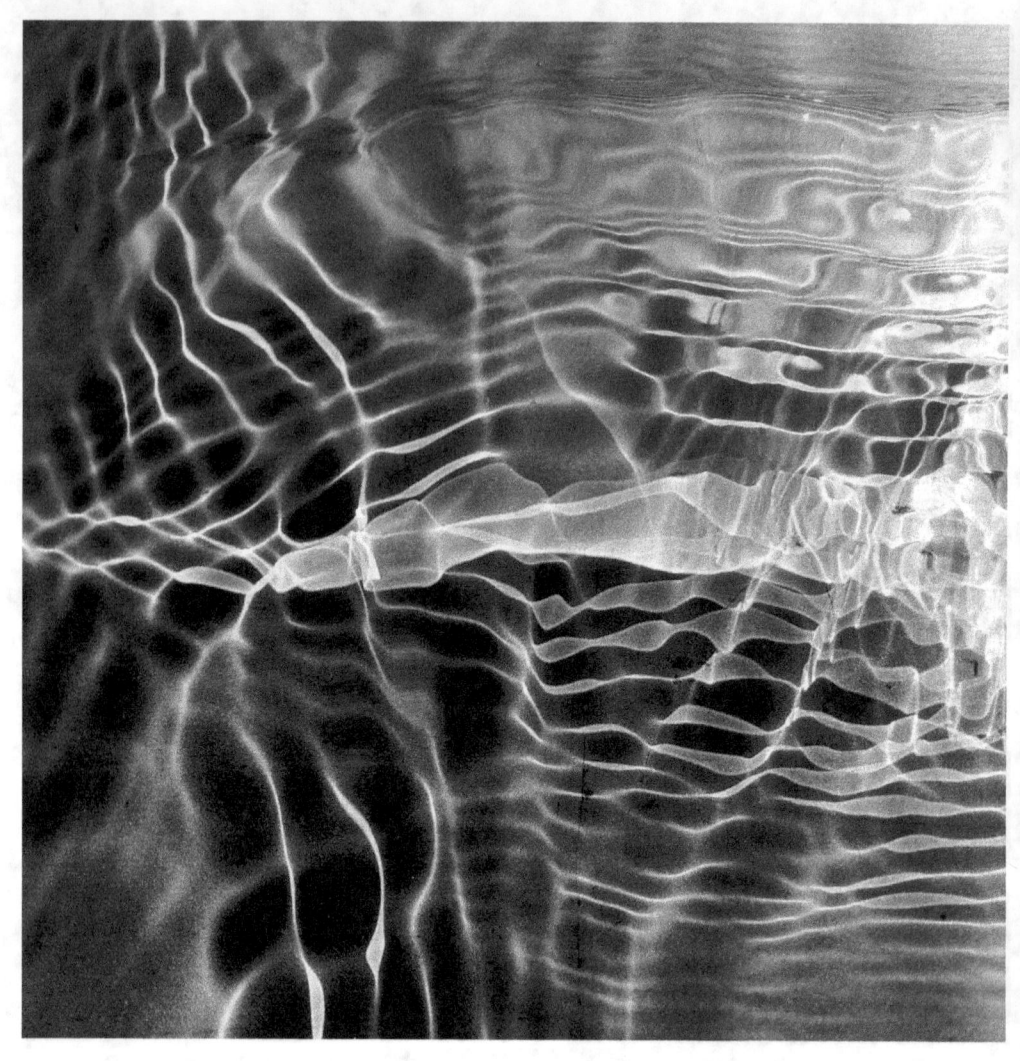

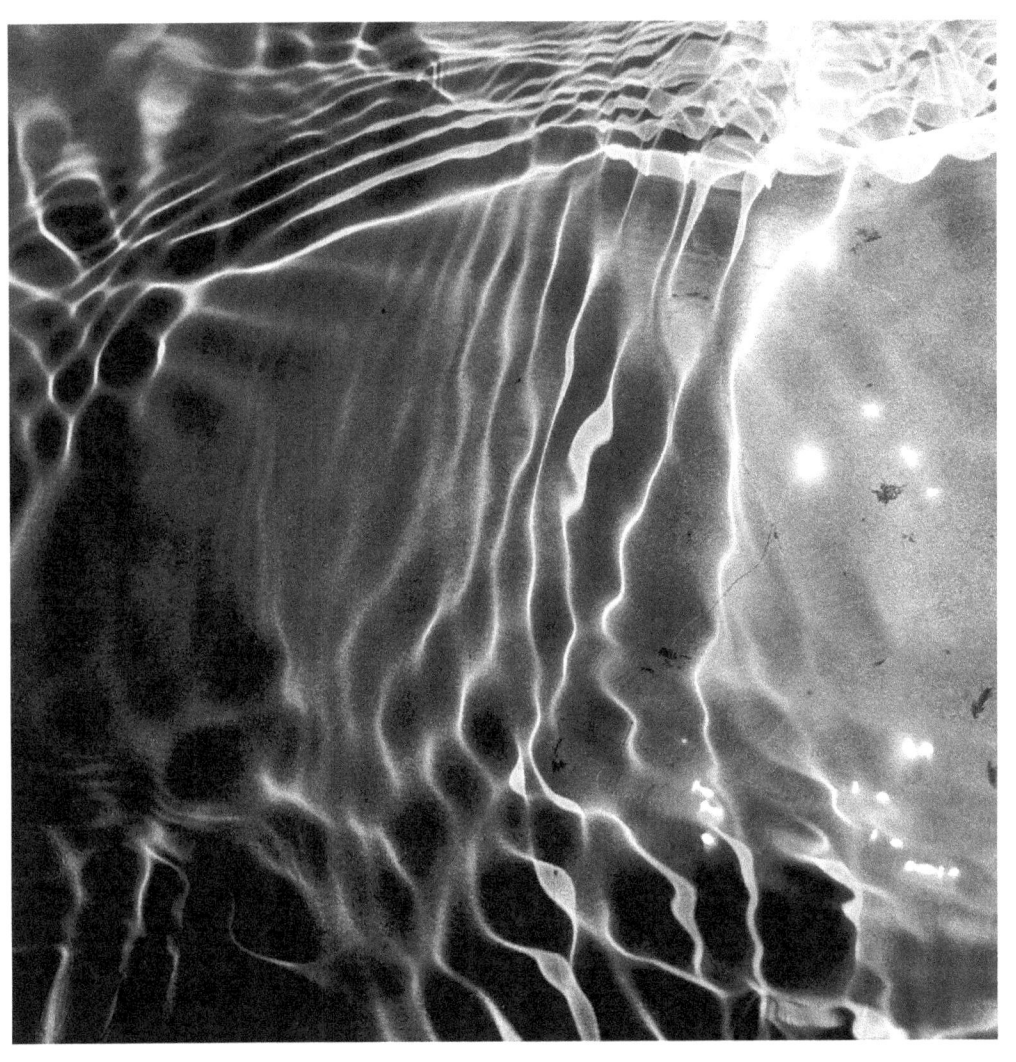

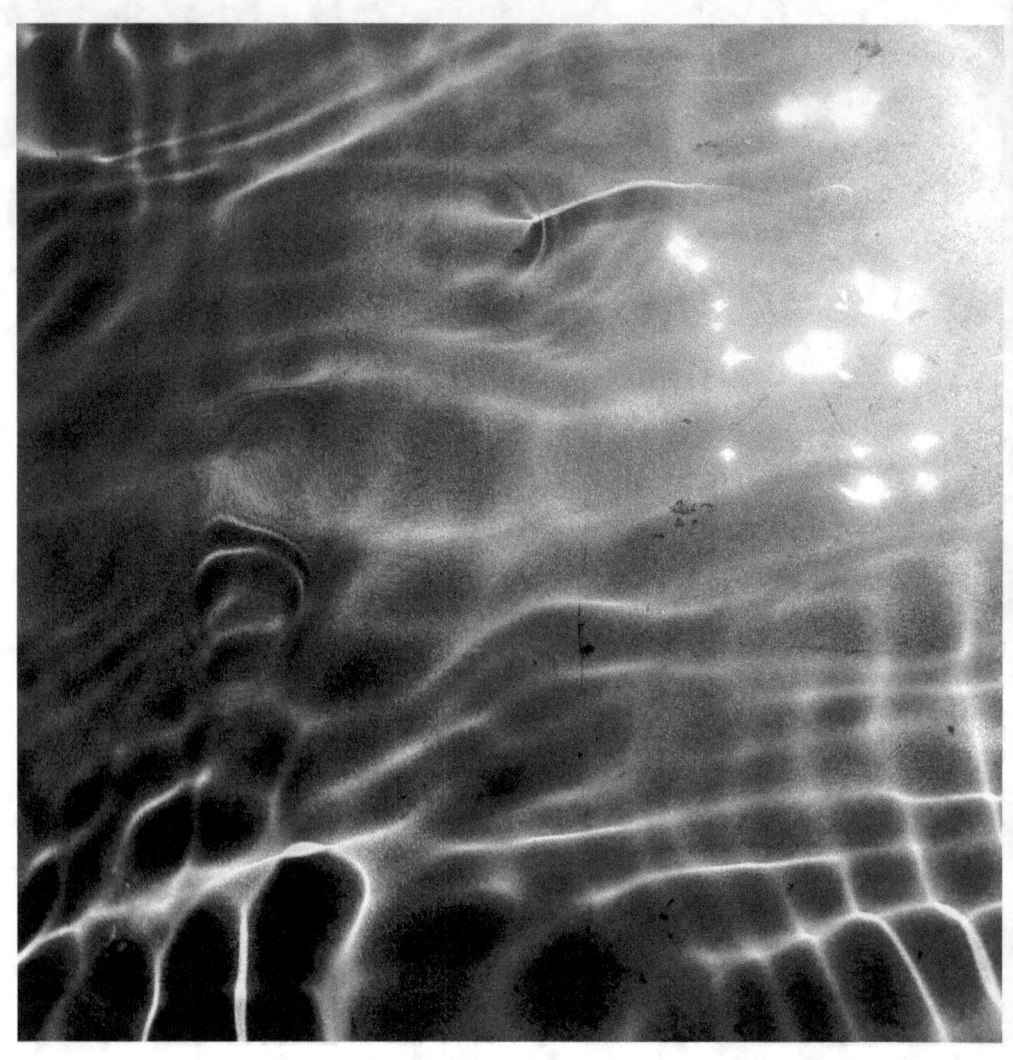

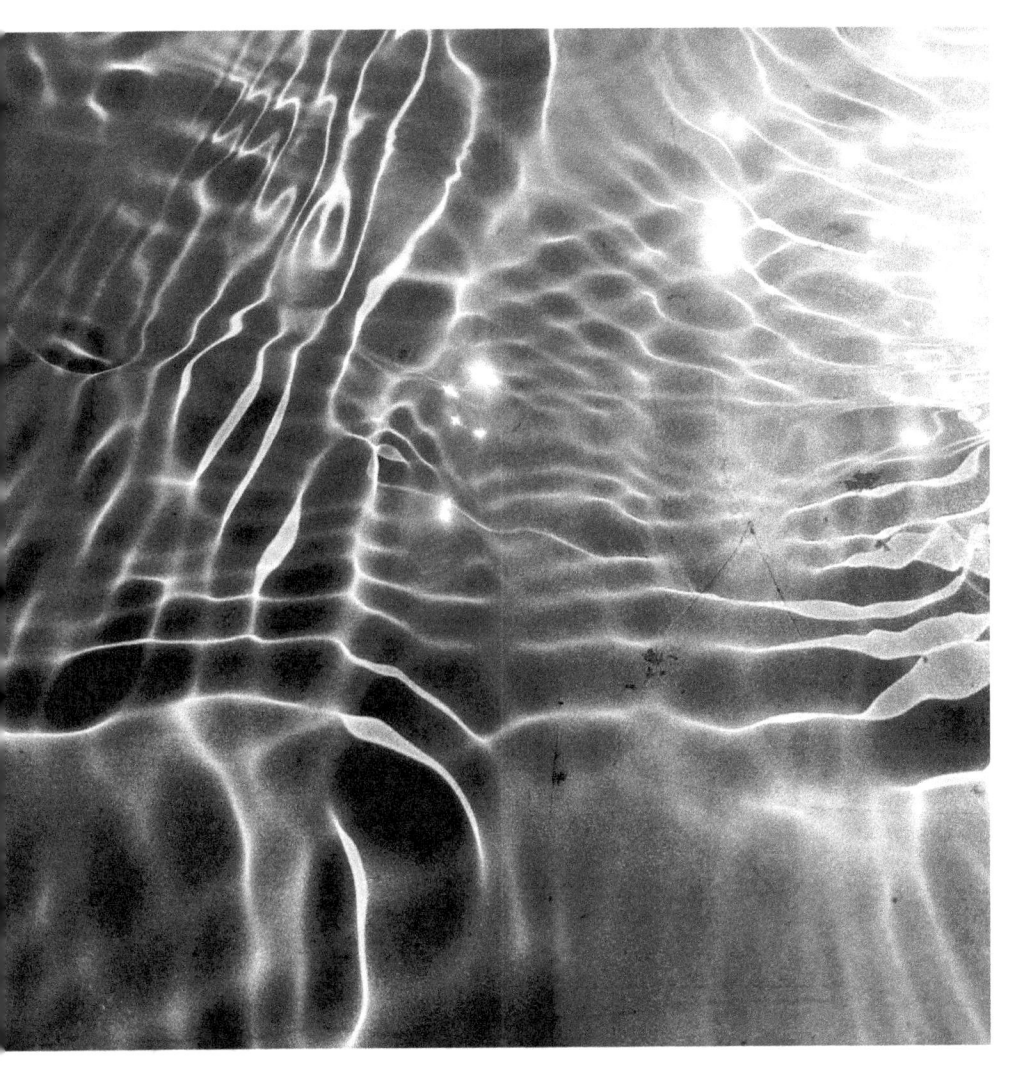

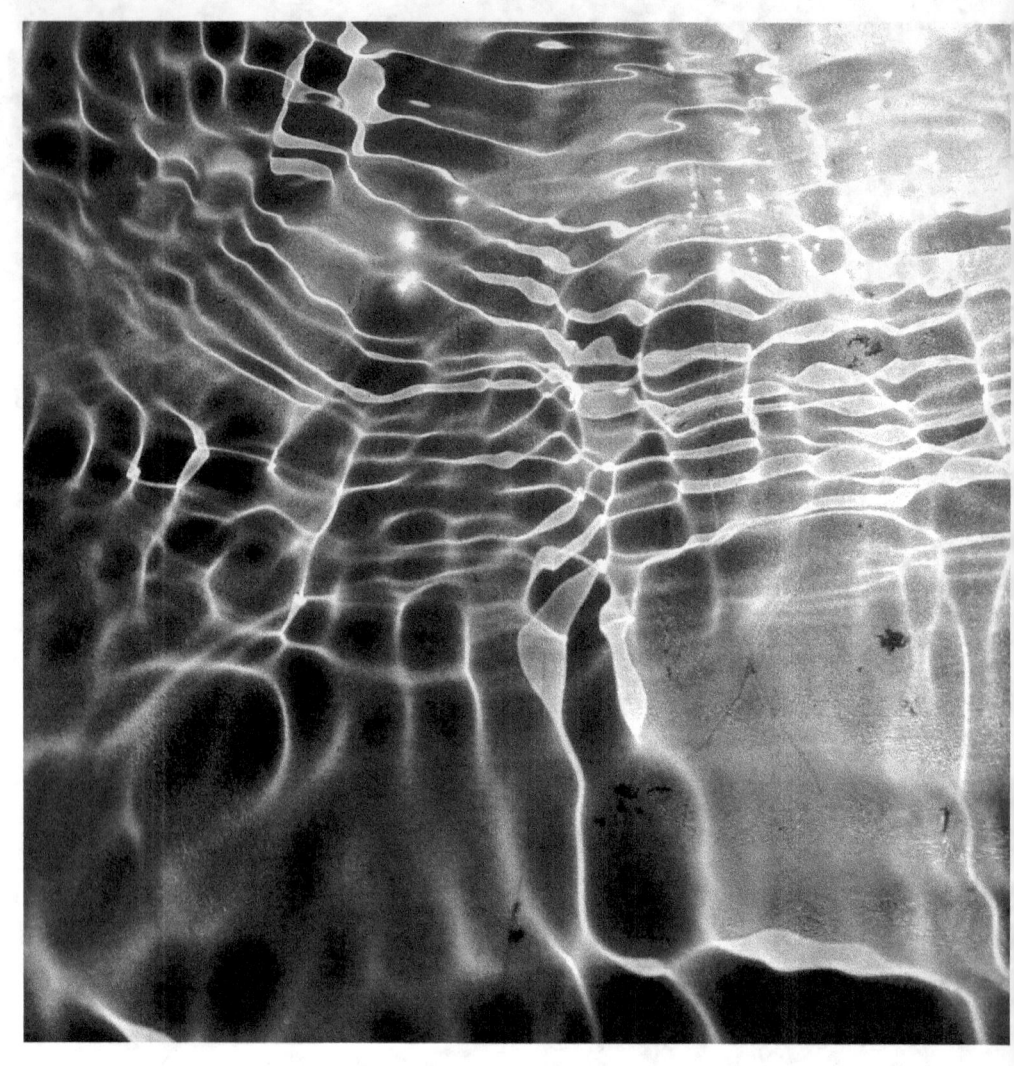

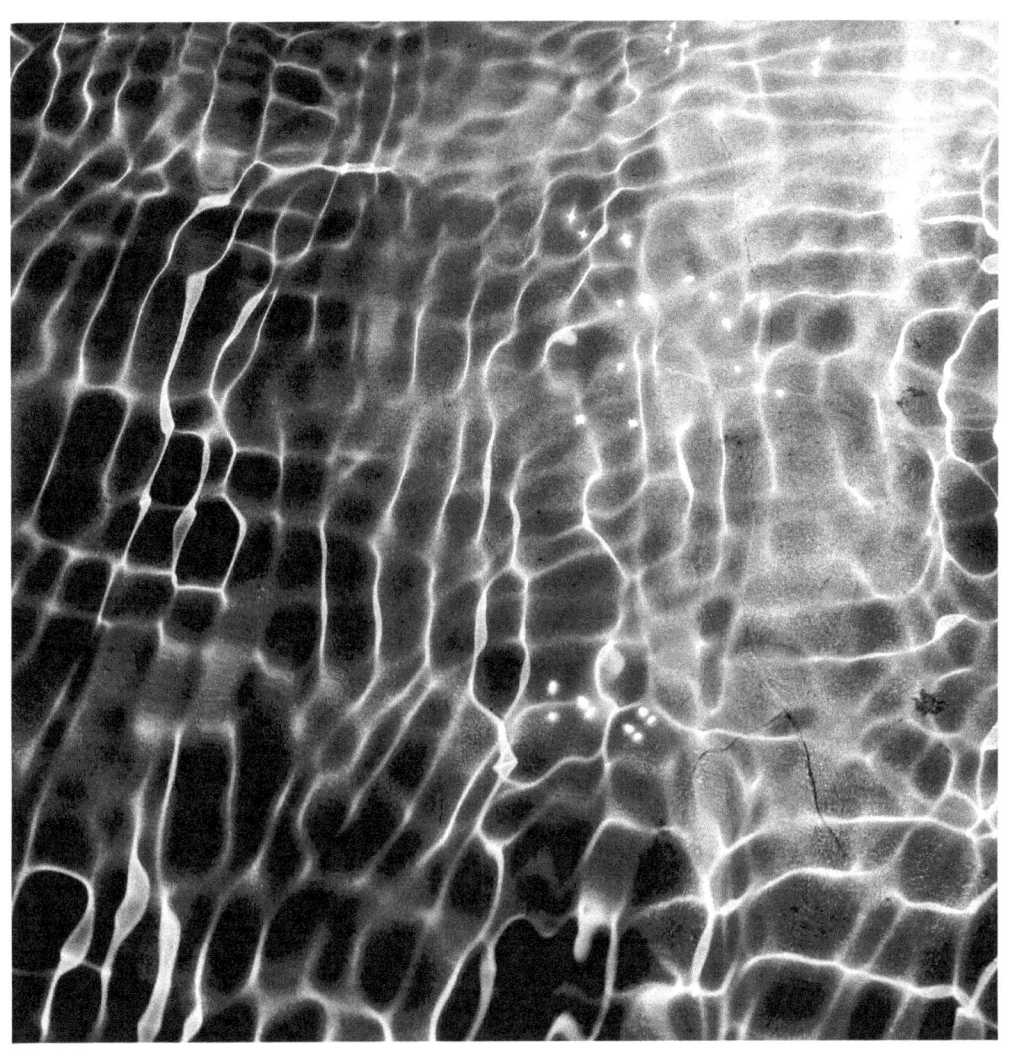

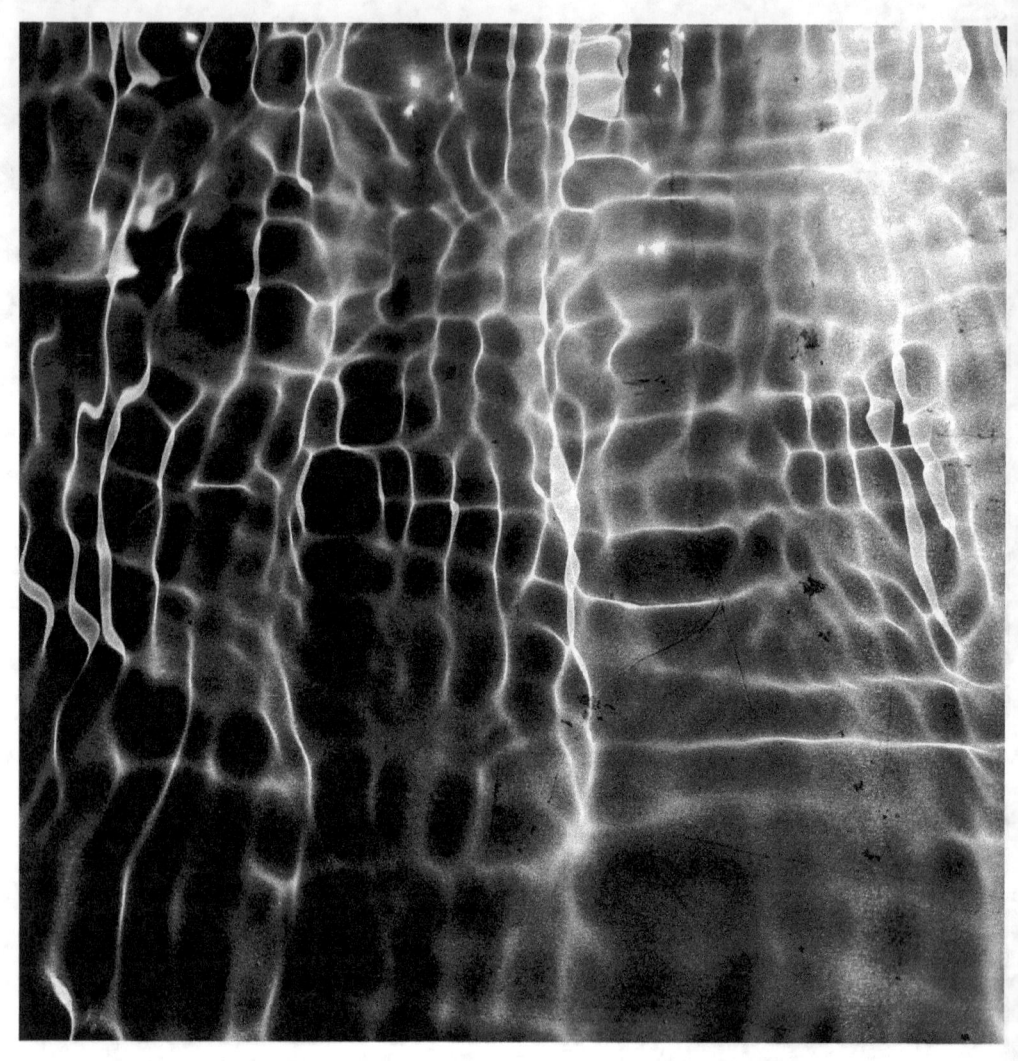

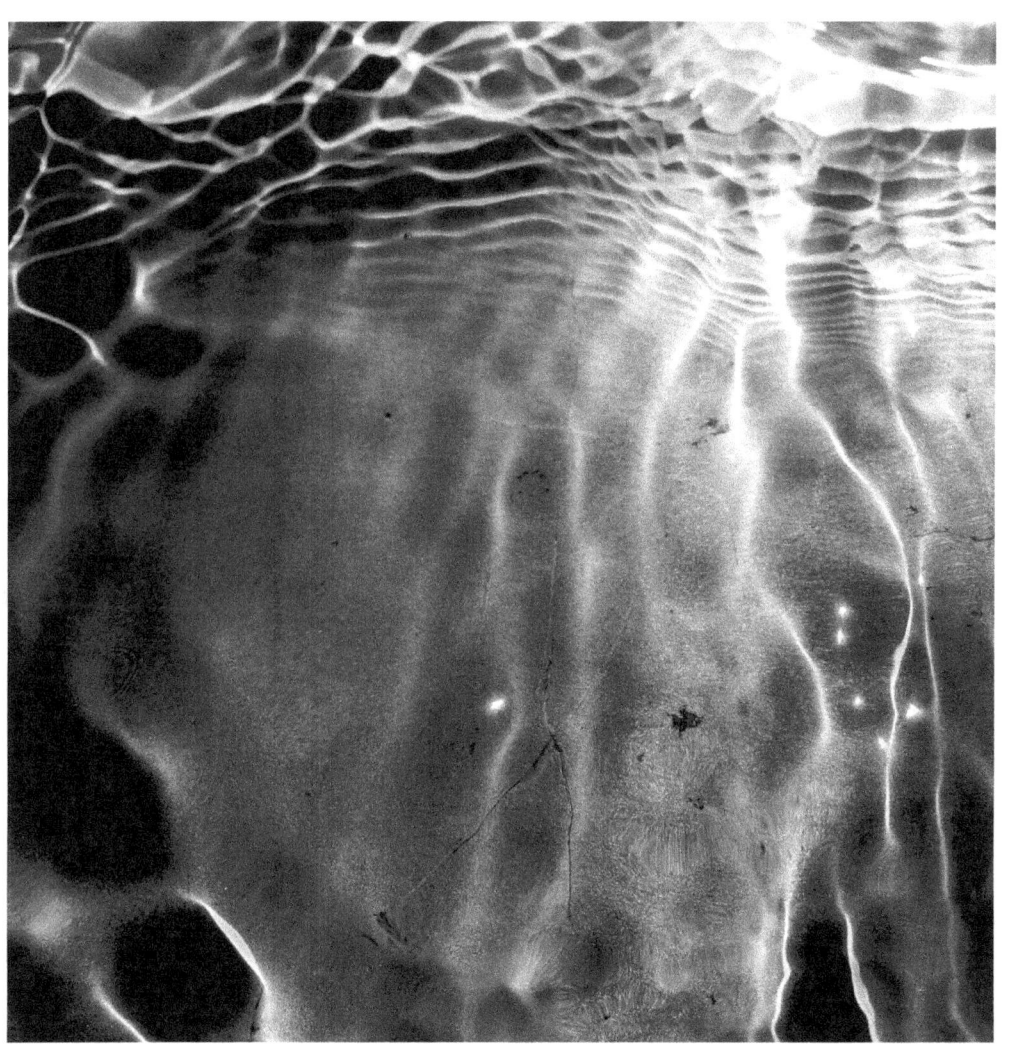

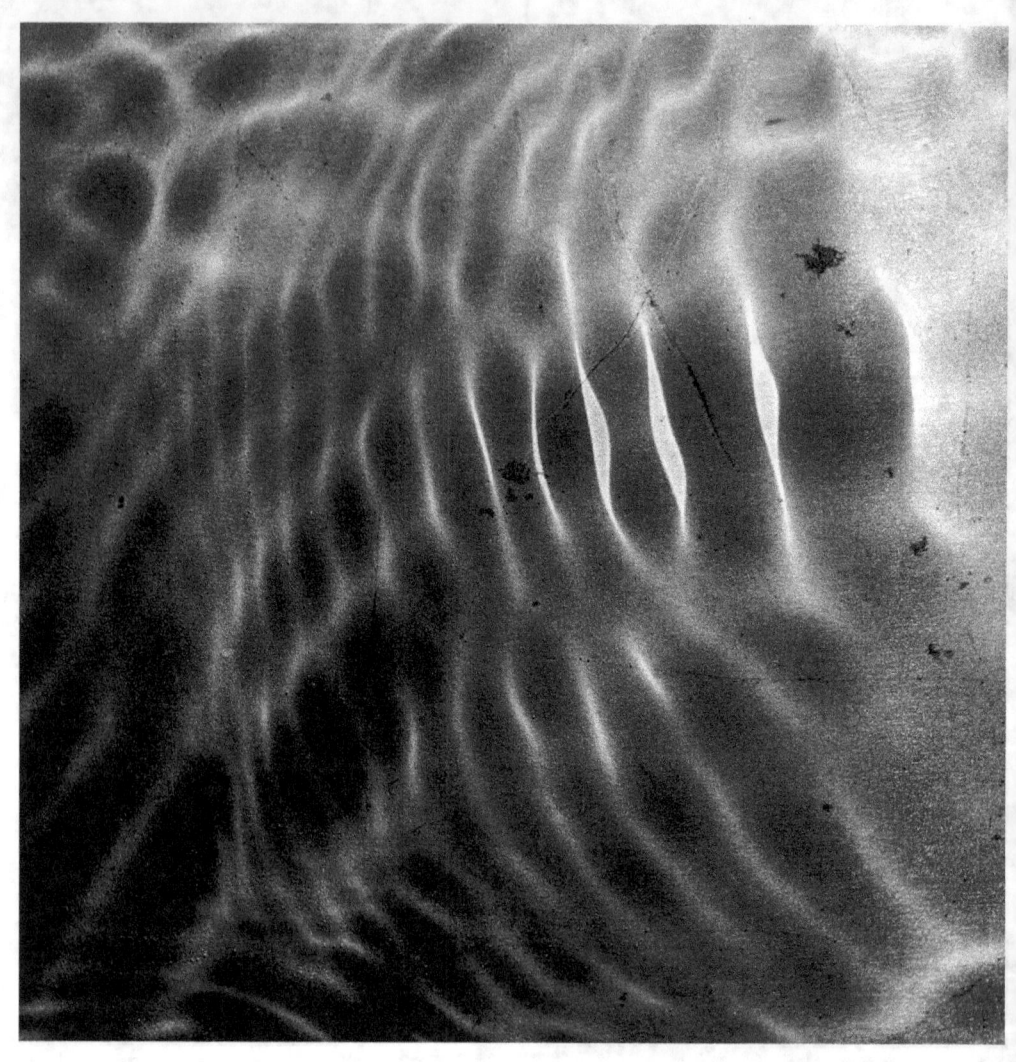

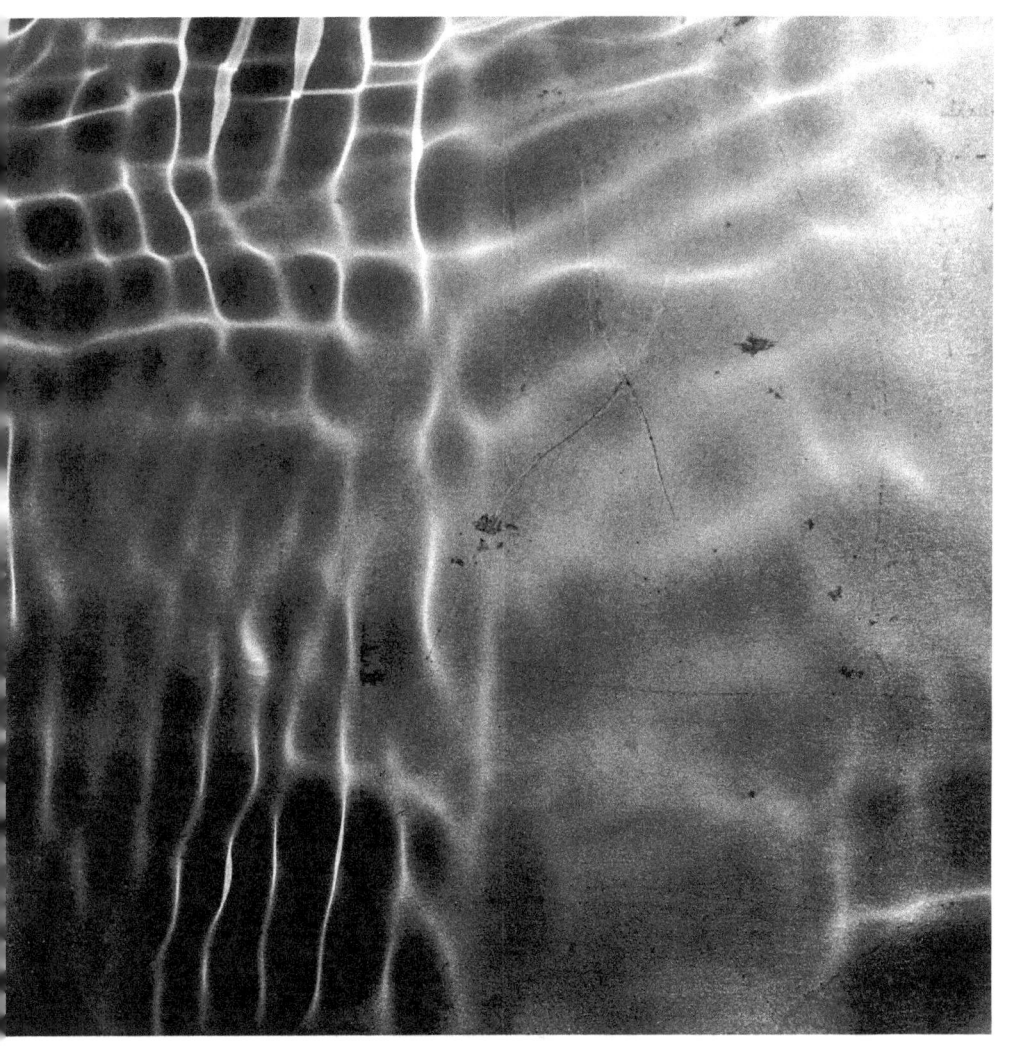

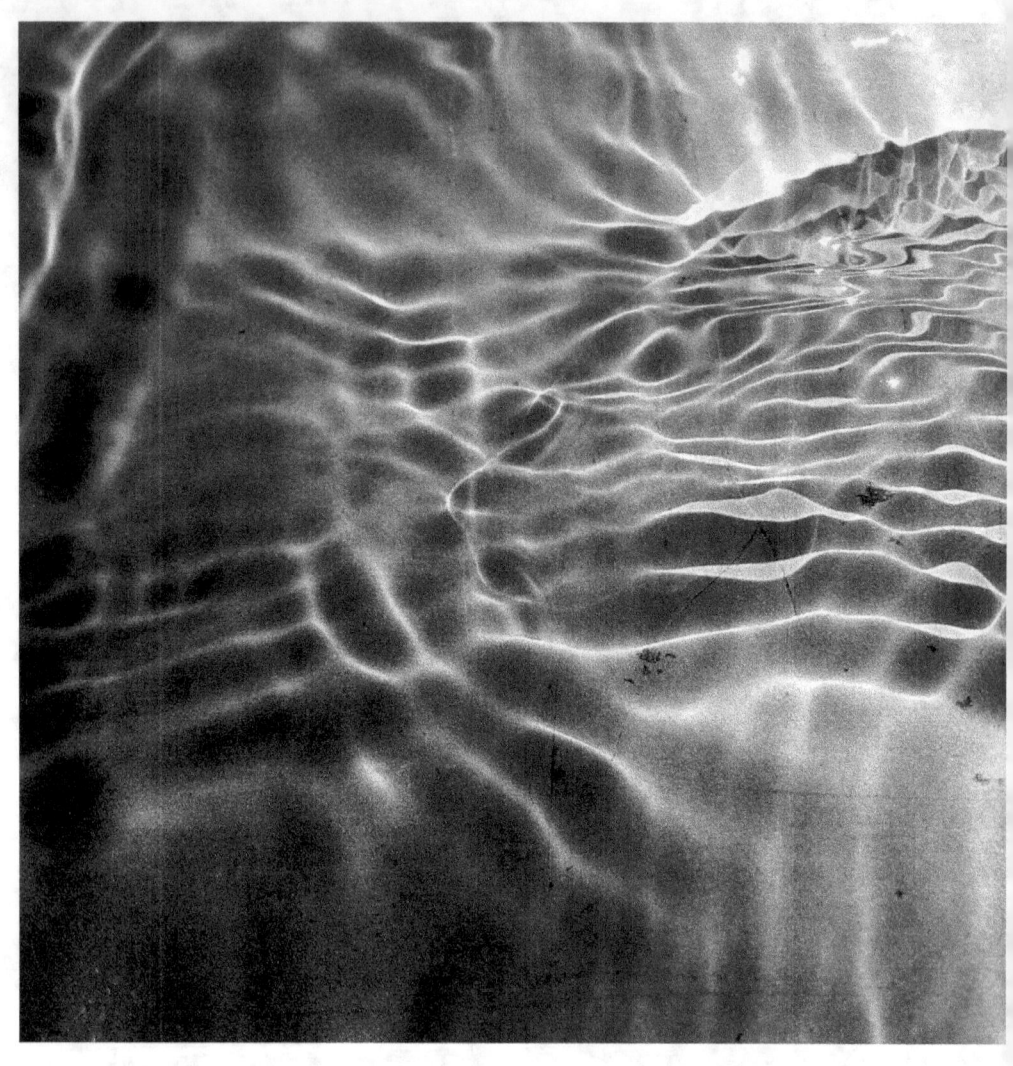

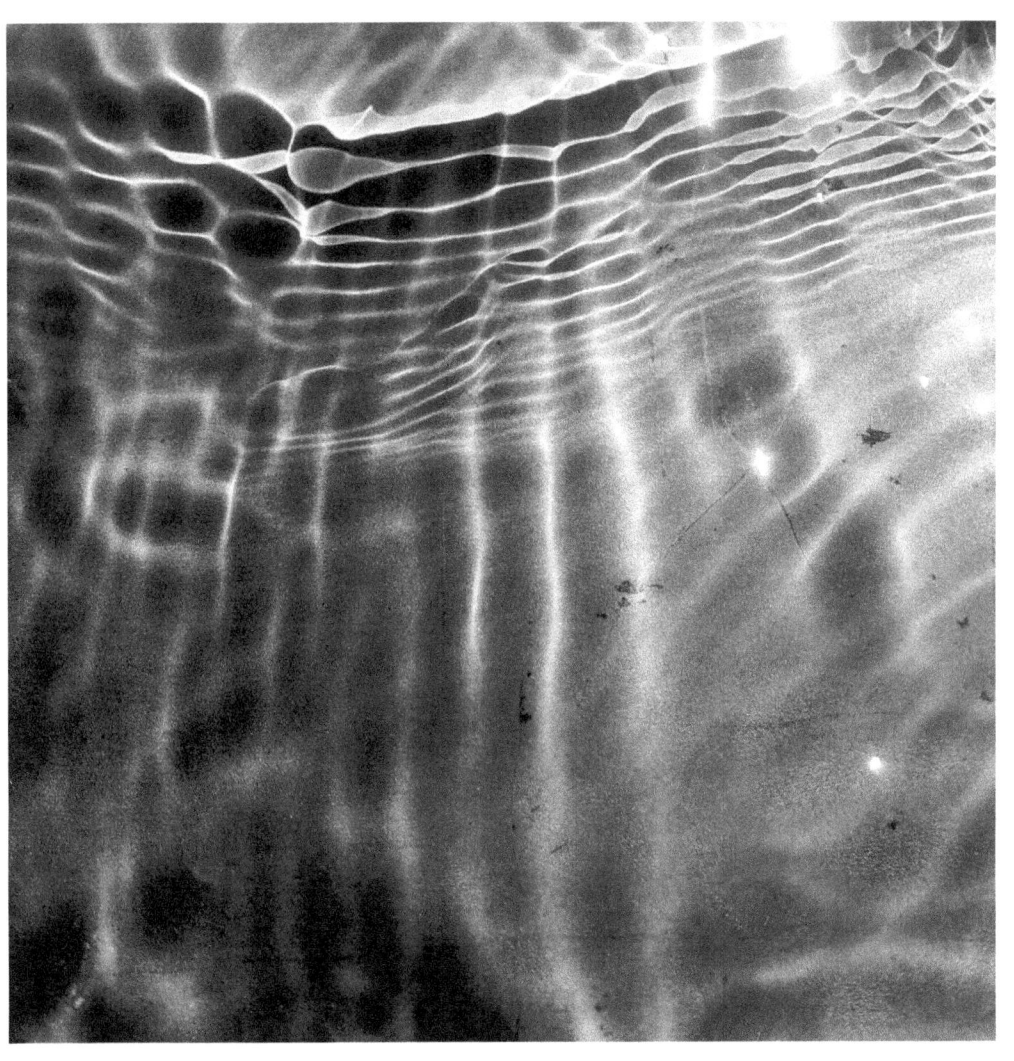

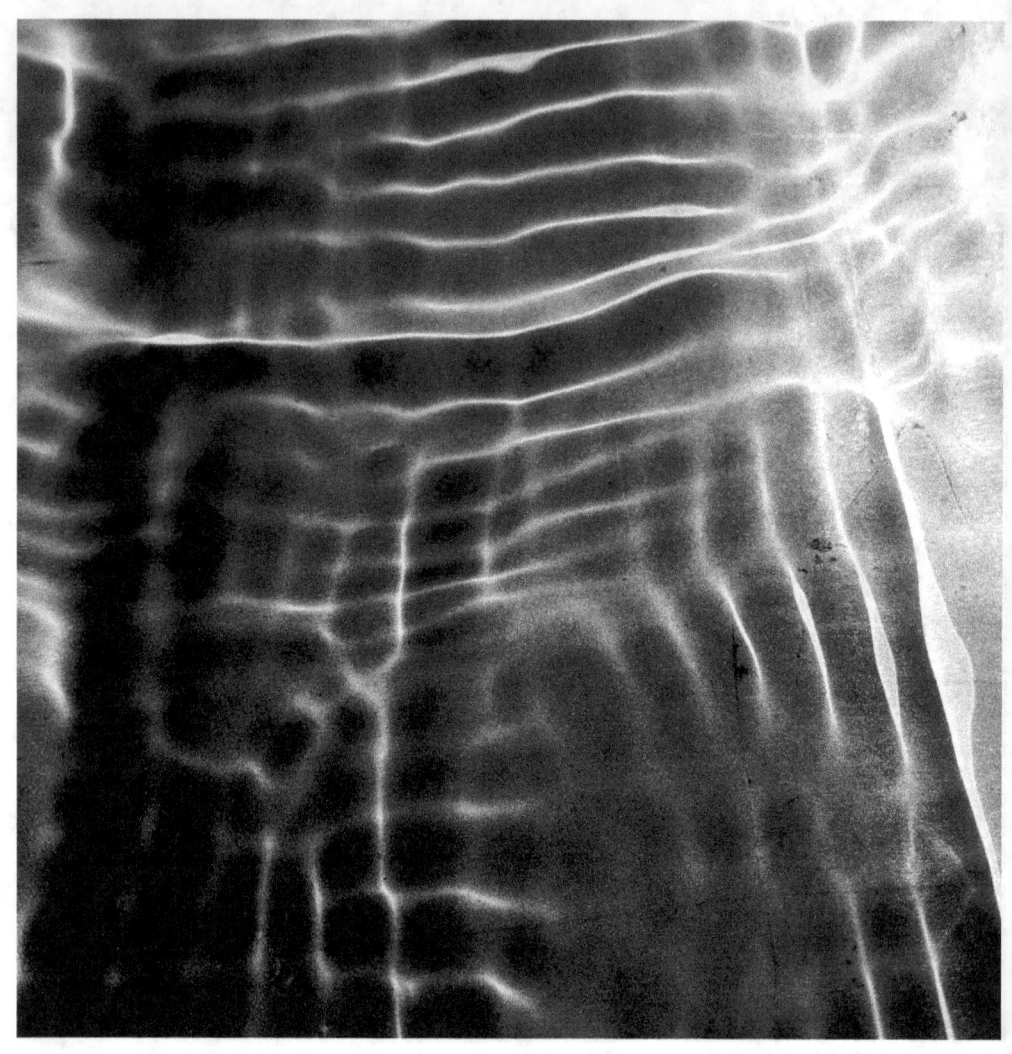

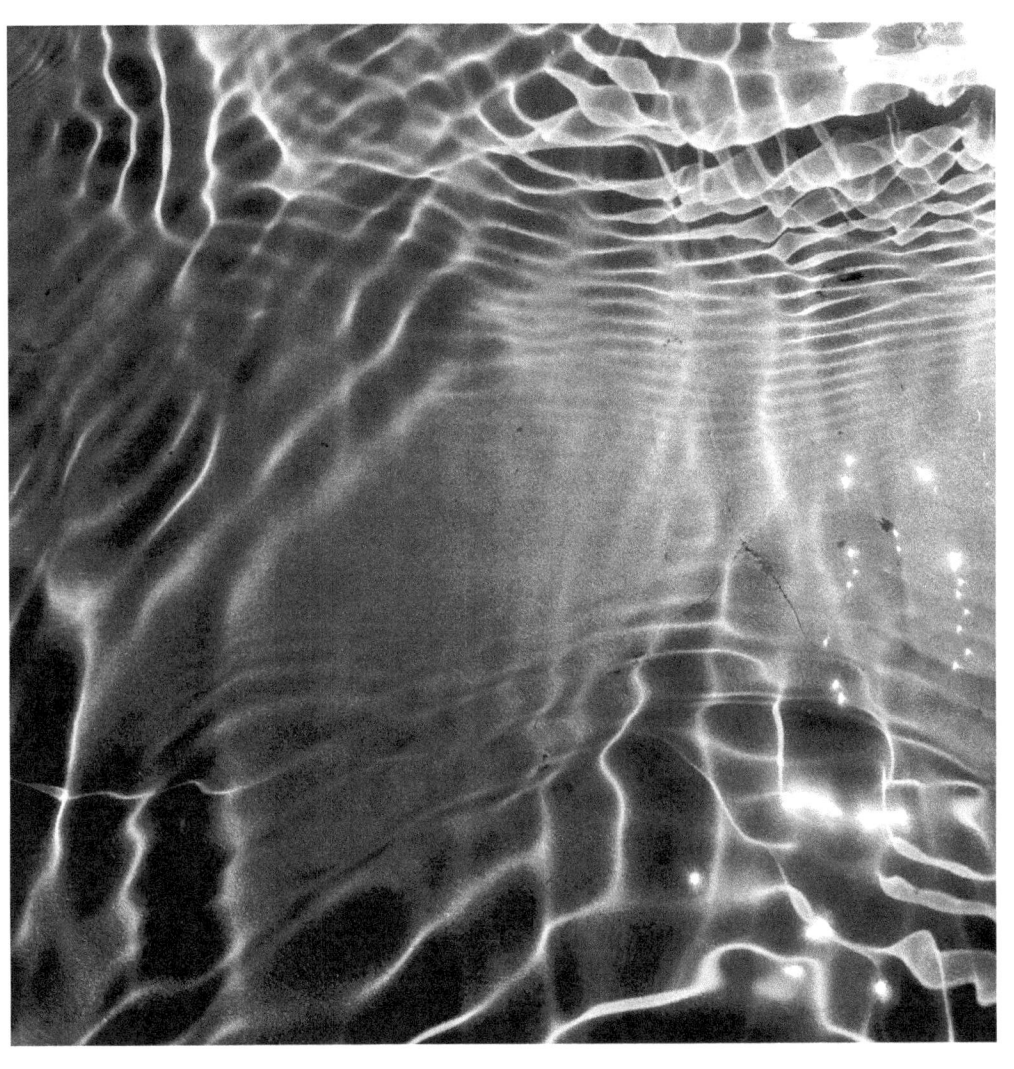

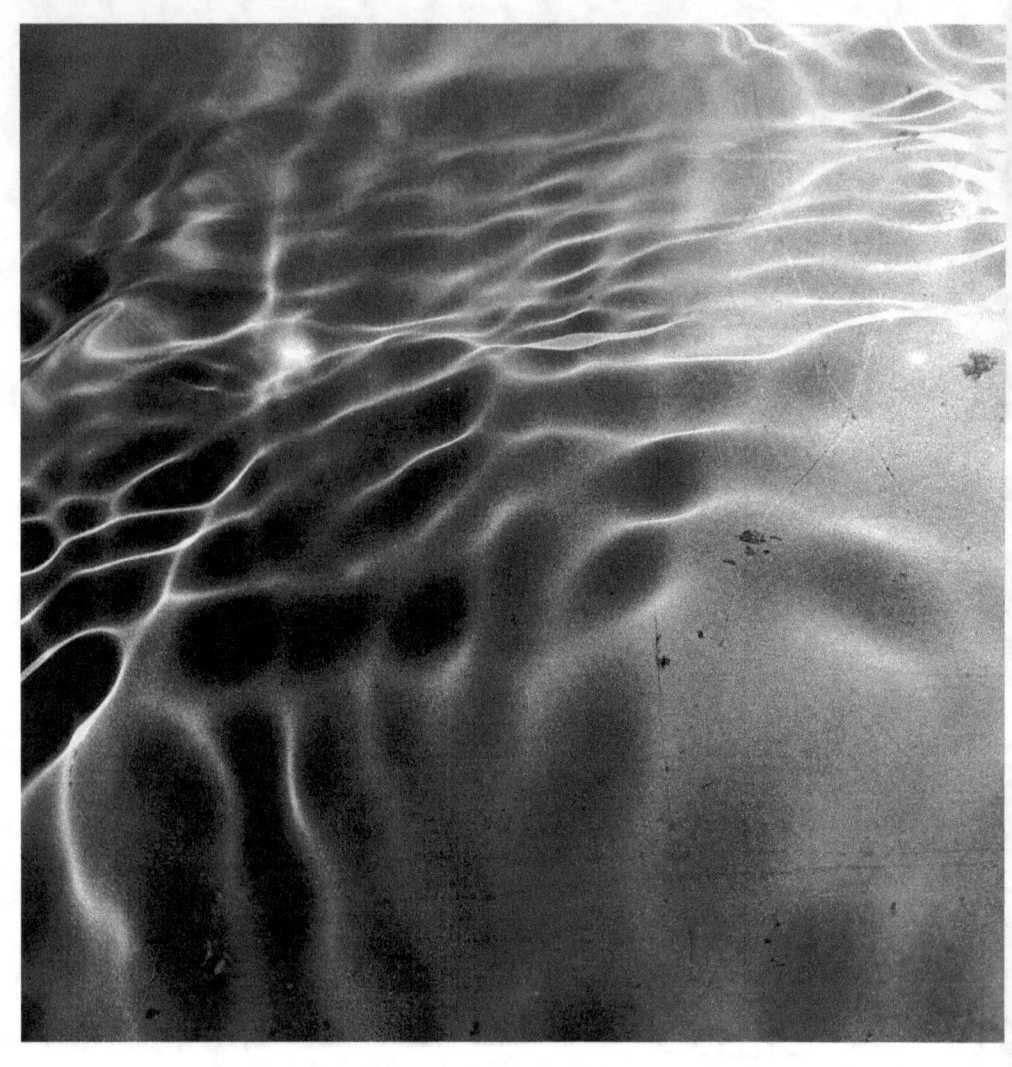

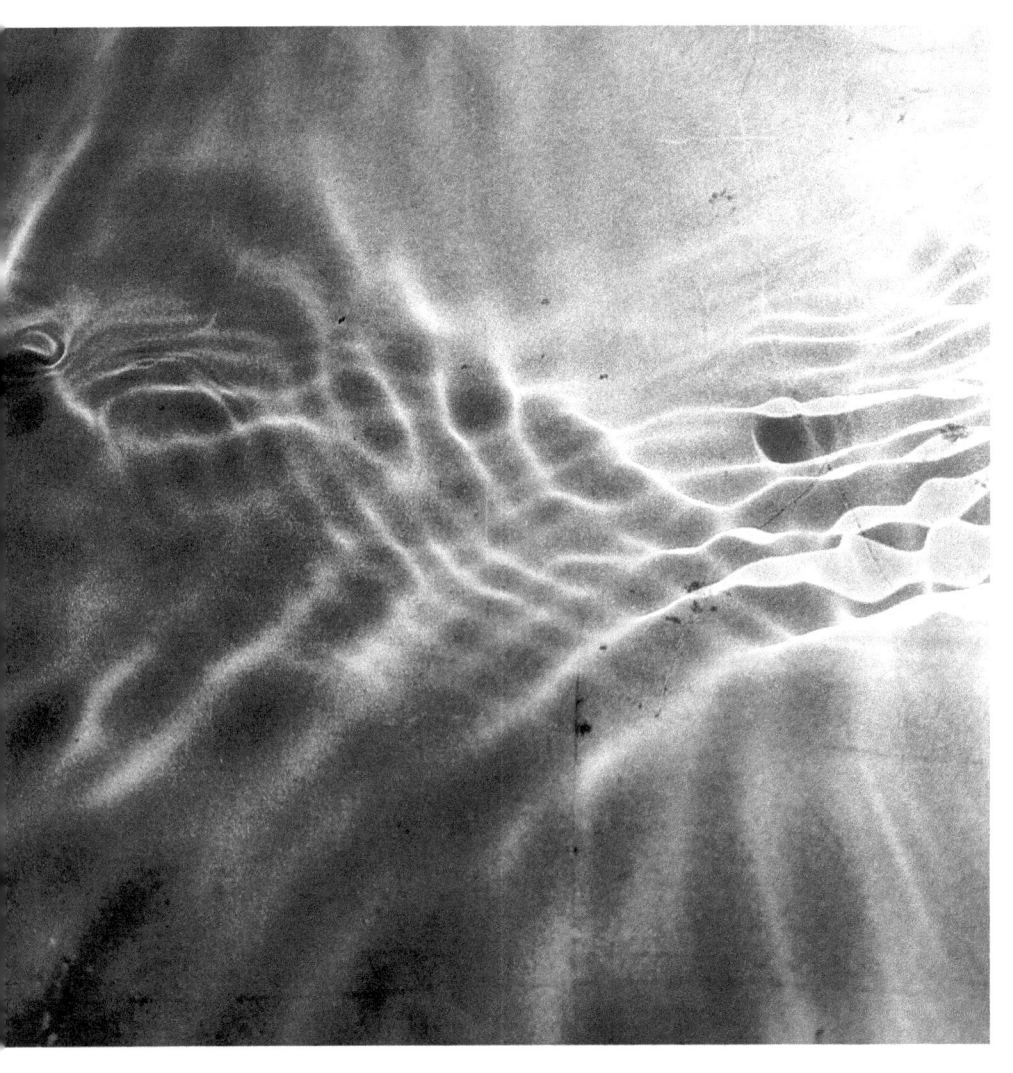

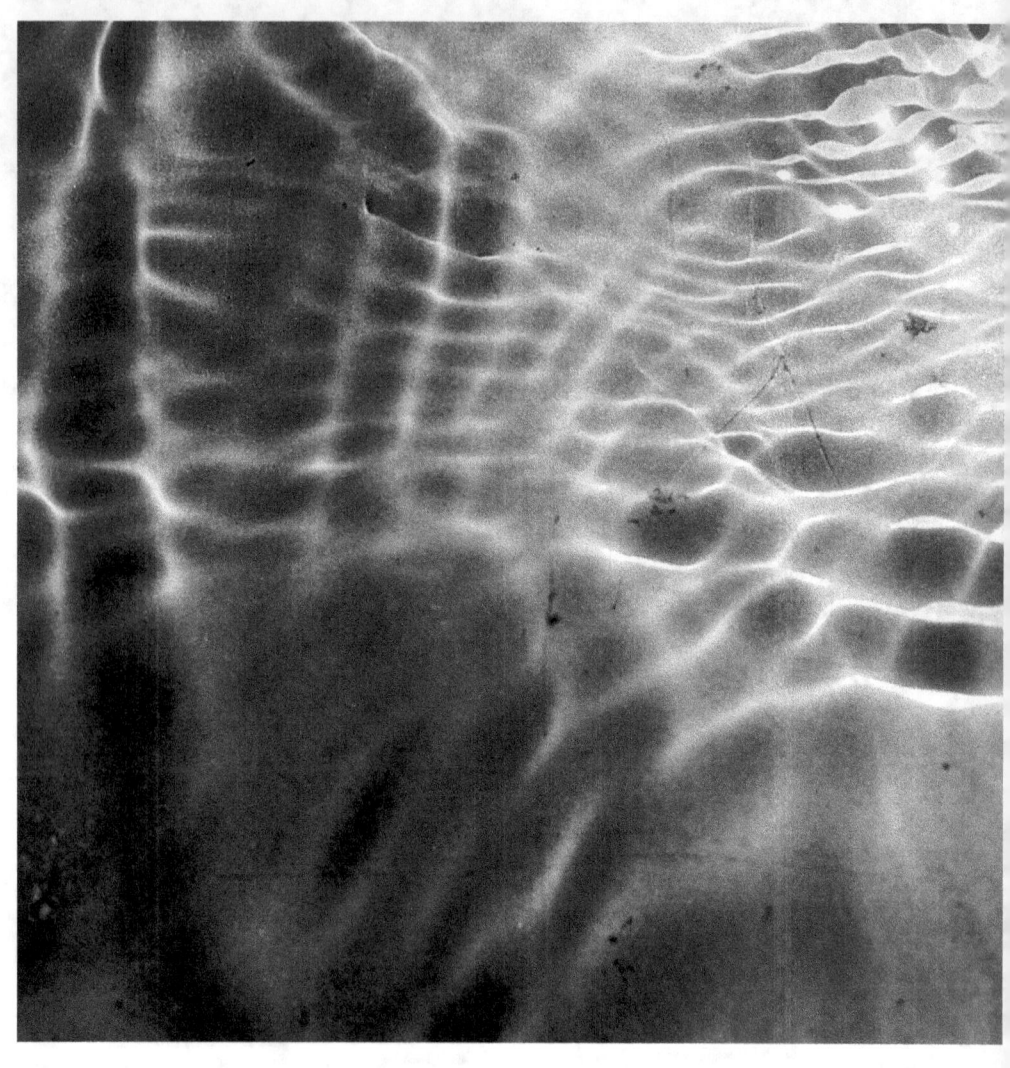

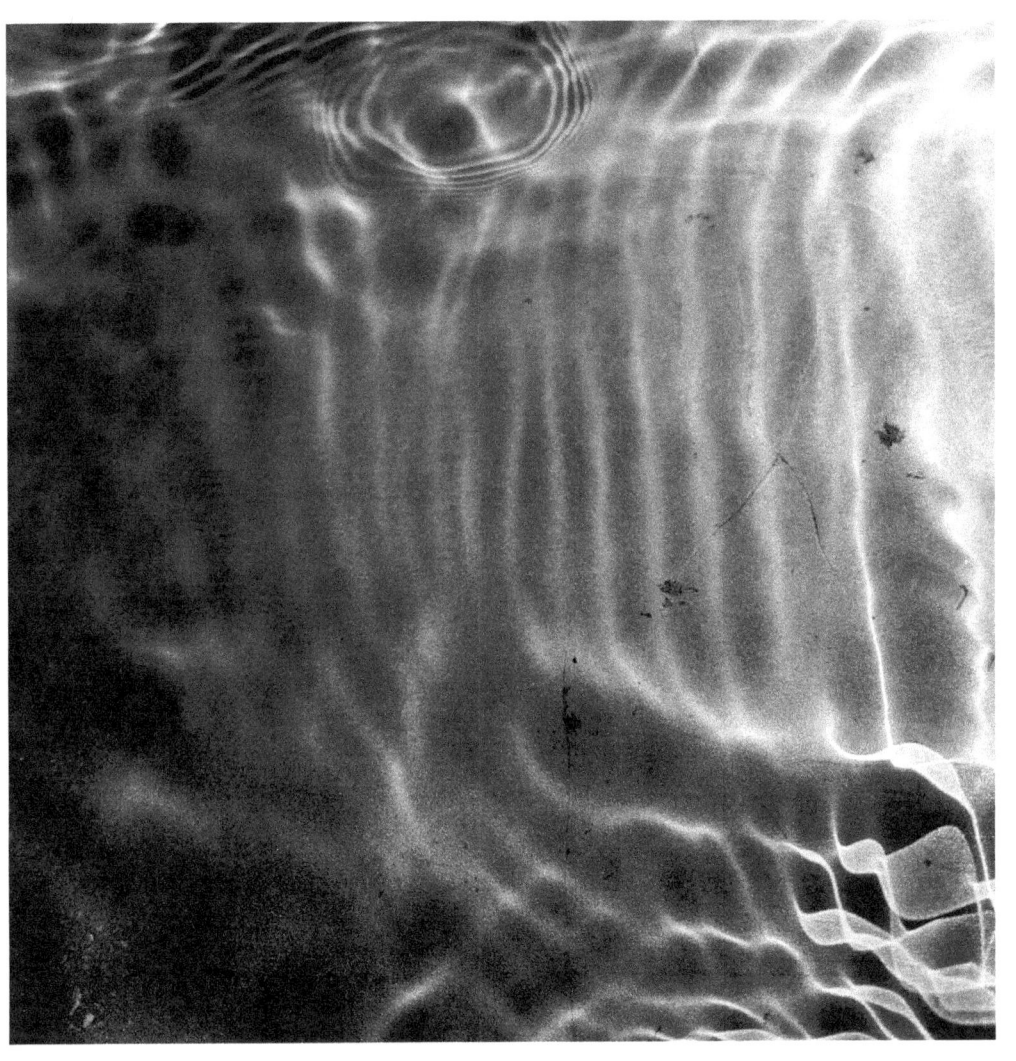

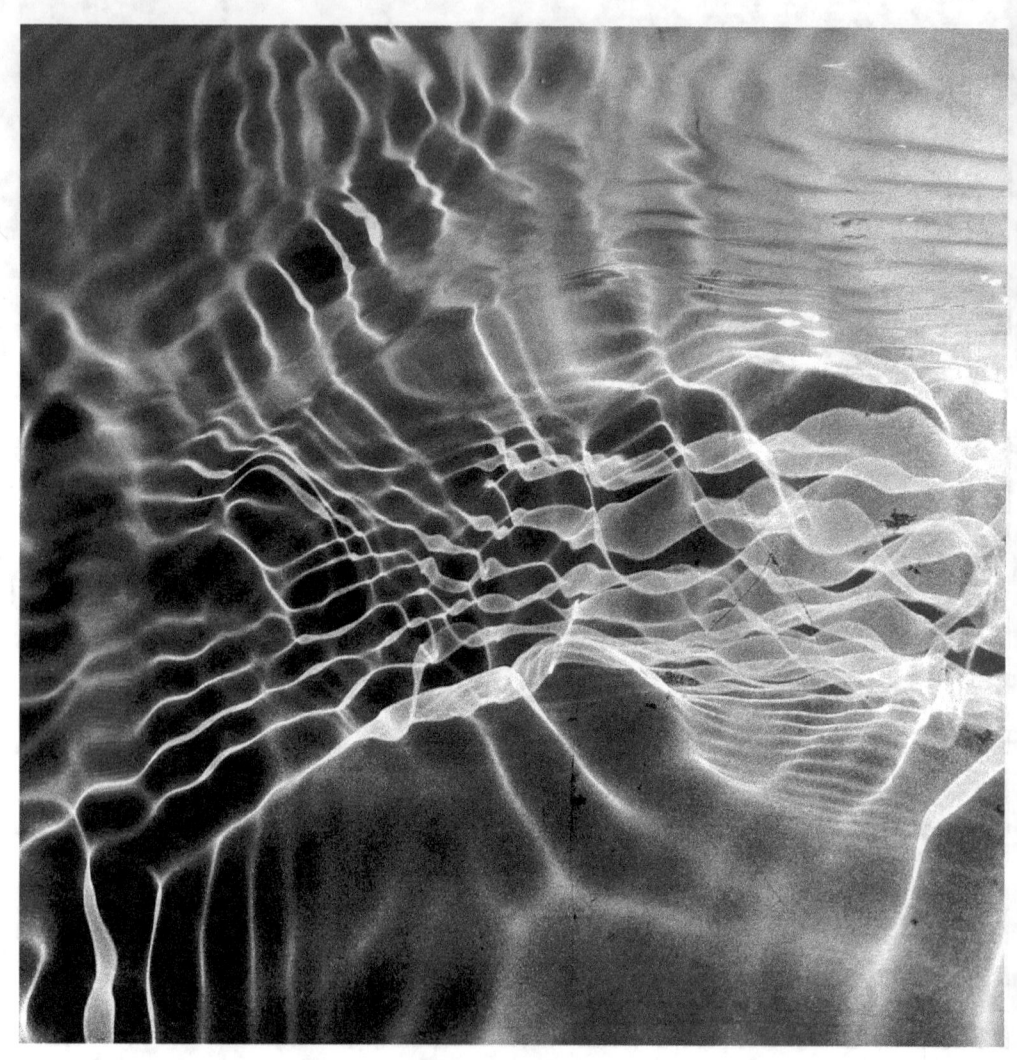